THROUGH IT ALL
the choice is rejoice

live wesige

Copyright © 2009 Live Wesige
All rights reserved.

ISBN: 1-4392-2384-X
EAN13: 9781439223840

Visit www.booksurge.com to order additional copies.

Through It All: The Choice Is Rejoice

Live's Biography

Outline of Contents

Chapter 1: The Lions Den 5

Chapter 2: Why the Name Live 15

Chapter 3: My Aunt, My Stepmother 29

Chapter 4: My Innocence Abused 39

Chapter 5: Over a Million Lost Their Lives 53

Chapter 6: Survivor in Exile 65

Chapter 7: Rebellious Teenager 79

Chapter 8: Redeemed and Born Again 93

Chapter 9: Conviction or Compromise 101

Chapter 10: Problems in Promises 117

Chapter 11: Minor Details of Life 129

Chapter 12: The Choice Is Rejoice 141

Acknowledgements

I could never have thought of writing a book if it weren't for God, who through the confirmations by many people inspired me to write this book.

I want to say thank you to my brothers; Placide Mizero, Denys Mubabo and Fiable Nibo; they have provided some pictures and reminded me of my stories I needed to write in this book. Thank you to my fiancé Claire Uwishema your love is a great treasure and a blessing to my life. Thank you to my adopted sisters and brothers Aline Umugwaneza, Alice Umulisa, Marcel Muyango, Adolph Rwandarugari, Nicole Ikirezi and Arthemon Mbaraga. Your lives are a testimony of God's goodness and through each of you I have learnt a lot that will help me in the future.

Thank you to the friends Dr. Felicien Rutayisire, Jean Desire Hullet, Richard Mugisha, Olivier Ngoga, Theophile Ngabonziza, Astelix Ndagijimana, Eddie and Lori Fargo, Thomas and Kari Mason, Garry and Beverley Moore, and Winston and Rebecca Chan, all of whom have stuck by me through thick, thin, and everything in between.

Thank you to the "parents" who did not accidentally appear in my life but were divinely appointed by God: Stanislas and Monique Sibomana, David and Donna Matejcek, Pastor Claude and Connie Tyler, Louis and M. Theresa Gakumba, Emmanuel and Vertha Nkunduwimye and Jean Bosco Rugangura.

Thank you to the ministers who stood by me during the writing of this book: Pastor Bernice Matejcek, Pastor Herbert. E and Juanita Crump, Pastor Rwigamba Albert and Ntagengwa Jean Baptiste's family and all the prayer warriors at Five fold ministry, Dayspring ministry, Zion Temple Celebration

Center Int'l, and Barbara Umuhoza. Thank you to the people who have recently entered my life with wisdom and humor: Etienne Masozera, Matt Johnson, Seth Eggesa, Maggie Jaruzel and Valentine Busogi. I hope I can return the gifts you've given me.

Thank you, God, for letting me keep my sanity and my memory long enough to finish this book. As I read over it for the thousandth time, I'm pretty impressed by how much of a life You've let me lead. Thank You for my story; I'm glad it all started with You.

To you reading this book, I hope you are entertained and learn a little more about me and what I've been through, and about how my choice is to rejoice at whatever happens in life. I hope you read the last page of this book liking me a little more and not too disappointed at my shortcomings but glorifying God at whatever you are going through.

So here is my story. Please read on and be filled with hope.

Introduction

My name is Live Wesige. I was born in Belgium, grew up in Rwanda, and now live in America. This book is a harvested seed of my past, which is now history; my present, which is a gift; and about God who holds the future as an untold mystery.

The experiences that make up my story are to some people an excuse not to believe in the existence of a creative, loving, and caring God, who is the master behind this life. The God above all others whose mercy and compassion kept me through it all Reminds me of this song:

I've had many tears and sorrows; I've had questions for tomorrow, there have been times I didn't know right from wrong. But in every situation God gave me blessed consolation that my trials come to only make me strong.

I've been in many places; I've seen many faces, there have been times I felt so all alone. But in my lonely hours, yes, those lonely times of my life, Jesus lets me know that I am His own.

Now I thank God for the mountains and I thank Him for the valleys, I thank Him for the storms He brought me through. For if I'd never had a problem, I wouldn't know God could solve them, I'd never know what faith in God could do.

(These words were inspired by God to Andrae Edward Crouch.)

This book is the result of all that happened in my life. The book *who are you? where are you going?* By Dr. M. Chandrakumar states a quote by Dag. H., "Philosophy theorizes about life. Psychology analyses life. History records life. Sociology classifies life. All men desire life. If life is a comedy to he who thinks, and a tragedy to he who feels, it is victory to he who believes in Jesus Christ." But Jesus said, "I am the life."

For this reason I testify that life is victory because I choose to believe. Through the ups and downs of this precious life, as a believer, my life has become a testimony of God's eternal purposes as well as each of us as individuals.

In the pages of this book, you are going to discover, as I did, that in order to be victorious in this life, first we must learn and understand that whatever happens to us is common. Second, we must all know that God is faithful, and third, we must never lose hope; there is a way of escape. After I understood these secrets of life, I can easily join the chorus of many others who sing the words "Through it all, through it all, I've learned to trust in Jesus, I've learned to trust in God. Through it all, through it all, I've learned to depend up on God's Word."

This is my story: through it all, the choice is rejoice.

Live Wesige

CHAPTER 1
The Lions' Den

Chapter 1: The Lions' Den

"Do you see the handsome man over there in the office? Who is he and where does he come from?" two ladies asked each other as soon as they saw Denys Zigama, a new government employee next door to their office.

The young man had observed the ladies while they whispered to each other; then he took a closer look at one of them. Finally, being bold, he got up and walked towards them. As he approached the office door he called out, "Caritas."

Both women were astonished to find out that this handsome man knew Caritas' name; this to them meant that he knew something about them both even though they had never met him. They were polite and warmly welcomed this unexpected guest.

Small talk started between Denys and Caritas, and soon they were no longer co-workers but friends and lovers talking about forming a family. Normally they would never have met, since both were from very rural, remote parts of the country, one from the west and the other the northeast, but their paths had brought them to Kigali, the capital city of the country of which both were citizens.

Let me write a little about the country. It is known as the land where "God spends His evenings," as they say in the Kinyarwanda language. It is a country that fully expresses the beauty of nature. Citizens and visitors alike call it "the land of a thousand hills" because of its geographical mountainous landscape. Rwanda is the country I'm speaking of. Those who know about Rwanda will also tell you the tribal conflicts of its people. My story begins with a couple among the many people who overlooked the ethnic walls that separate and

CHAPTER 1: The Lions' Den

bring division within our nation. The couple I'm talking about disregarded their tribal differences, married, and formed a family. They were my parents.

A few months after their first acquaintance in the office, they began to date, and in just few months discovered that they were meant to be together. So when Denys proposed marriage the beautiful Caritas couldn't wait any longer. She immediately said yes. But in Africa, the families still have the last say concerning the marriage of their children. Even though these adults both loved each other, they still had to consult their parents over that decision. Oh! I'm glad their parents were supportive.

In Africa, in my country to be specific, once the families accept their children's marriage, the family of the boy will come to ask the family of the girl about the date to pay the dowry. That same date will be the day for a traditional wedding, after which the two lovers are now considered and acknowledged as engaged not only by the family but also by the community. The traditional wedding is a big party event. But even though the engagement takes place, the decision to get married can be canceled if one of the lovers finds out something that he/she can't tolerate. That's how it used to be even though the civil wedding was a week or months apart. These days some people prefer to do both at the same day due to a shortage of funds or time.

Sometimes the marriage proposal is canceled based on tribalism, say for example Hutu or Tutsi families refusing to have intermarriage. Among many other reasons for canceling the marriage proposal is social class, the rich refusing in-laws of a poor background! Huh! Silly but true.

Anyway, back to the couple Denys and Caritas. On November 14, 1981, they made their vows to become one. Their marriage celebration was one of a kind; I'm talking about a ceremony that their families, relatives, friends, and co-workers attended and where all ate and drank liberally. Believe me, in Africa weddings are expensive since you don't know the number of people to expect. Most often the number is more than expected because a friend invites another friend. Sometimes people who are not invited just invite themselves, so this makes it fun but expensive! But there is a belief that once there is much to eat and much to drink, then the party is a success.

My parents' wedding was very much so. They even had a wedding cake! Oh, come on, don't take it for granted; we are talking about Africa, where some people don't even know what bread is! But my parents' wedding was amazing.

Life after their wedding was full of adventures, as both were adventurous. They would go places to see the beauty of Rwanda. They saw mountain gorillas, which are only found in the volcanic mountain forests of the country. They went swimming in Lake Kivu many miles away from the city where they lived. They organized parties, most especially on Christmas and New Year's Eve. They made more and more friends, as my father was getting wealthier. They took these times of fellowship so seriously that every lunch time they met just to talk and share food. In the evenings, once their office driver dropped them at home, they would go jogging, and each time they ended their jogging session with a love kiss on the cheek. Neighbors envied them, but all of this was of no concern to my parents, who had a world of their own where their love for each other was strong.

CHAPTER 1: The Lions' Den

During their leisure time Dad played soccer while Mom played basketball. Both were members of their office teams and were good at what they loved. They were very athletic, and what's more amazing is that both of them were fans of volleyball. There was no doubt that things were only going to get better for them as a couple, and in just a year they were blessed to bring the first fruits of their love into the world, a healthy baby boy. They named him Placide Mizero, a name that means hope for a continued happiness in the future.

A few months after the birth of their firstborn, it was time to take the child to show the grandparents, as is our culture. In this case Mom's parents lived in the home where she grew up in the western part of the country.

Rwanda is divided into provinces, and my mother's province is Gisenyi. They flew to get into Gisenyi and then drove to her grandpa's, although this city is within driving distance; but flying was for adventure. The visit to my mother's parents was another joyous time for the family, and from there they decided to take a trip to the former province of Byumba in the northeast. That way my father's parents would be able to see their grandson.

A year later, Mom was again pregnant, and they planned a picnic visit to their family friends, Mr. and Mrs. Butera. They traveled with one of Dad's best friends Bosco and headed toward the east, the location of Rwanda's Akagera National Park. Little did they know that this trip was a turning point in their lives, because everything that happened after this trip was a disaster for my family

The following is a testimony, a story that has eyewitnesses, so please don't think it's fictional. No! It is an encounter of God's own miraculous hand of protection. You might have read in the Bible about Daniel, who was thrown in the lions' den due to the total trust that he had put in God. According to the Bible, the Almighty Creator of the universe was able to rescue Daniel from those dangerous, hungry, angry lions. The full story is available in Daniel 6:1-22. I have come to the understanding of Daniel's story as I relate it to mine!

It was 1983 in the moonlight of the twenty-sixth day of October around eleven p.m. My dad, mom, one-year-old brother Placide, and Bosco the family friend were traveling back home from their picnic visit to the eastern part of our country, the country of a thousand hills in the great lakes region of the central part of Africa.

As they traveled across Akagera National Park, they met a group of deer crossing the road that divided the parklands in two; the deer were running to escape lions that had their stronghold at the rock of Karangazi. At this rock, lions attack and kill both people and animals.

My father tried to dodge these deer but the car slid and rolled away from the road. My father and his friend Bosco were able to jump out, but Mom, who was pregnant, was trapped inside the rolling vehicle with Placide.

The car slid and rolled until it was stopped by one of the big cave stones of the lion's den. Although she was severely injured and couldn't move her legs, Mom pushed herself out and pulled Placide out from the wrecked car; but by the time they got out lions were surrounding the car. A lioness that had just produced cubs took my brother away, maybe thinking that he was a cub, and she stopped the other lions from getting any closer. As Mom watched this scene helplessly, she lost consciousness.

CHAPTER 1: The Lions' Den

Two hours later, a truck of soldiers passing by stopped, and the driver volunteered to get a rescue team from the nearby Gabiro guesthouse, where there was a group of soldiers.

Hallelujah, the lioness had not harmed my brother! My mother, though still unconscious and severely injured by the accident, was also unharmed by the lions. The soldiers came on time! A miracle! The lioness saw the rescue team and brought my brother back. We were saved and spared by the Almighty God. My mom was seven months and three weeks pregnant with me, and this was only the beginning of many miracles that lead to the story in this book. God is always there, even when He seems to be silent.

This picture is my parent's wedding on November 14, 1981 at the reception.

THROUGH IT ALL: The Choice is Rejoice

This picture is my mother holding Placide arriving at a local airport during their visit in Gisenyi.

CHAPTER 2
Why The Name Live?

Chapter 2: Why The Name Live?

Hallelujah! God is great. I'm still amazed by His love and protection against any harm caused by the lioness at the lion's den. This contributed to a series of events culminating with my miraculous birth, and my naming.

As it is well known, parents are the most important influence in the development of a child's self-concept and personality. Thus, their name is probably the first of such messages children receive from their parents.

There are many factors or patterns to giving a child his or her name. Family tradition is an important factor. Another naming pattern is the use of names that are highly fashionable or popular, in other words, fad names. The third category reveals something about the personalities of the parents. These names are fanciful and bizarre, like Lastchance or Truckstop (a name once given to a boy because he was born in one). Some names indicate whimsical, highly individualistic, and exhibitionists personalities. On the other hand, names of this type may well result from lack of education, imagination, intelligence, or even all three. In some cases, these names may even be expressions of hostility towards the unwanted economic burden the child represents to the parents. There are some examples in the Bible like Jabez who was so named because he was born out of his mother's pain; his name meant *sorrow and trouble* (1 Chronicles 4:10). Parents should remember that their child's name will always have an effect on his or her life.

Well, my name, Live, is pretty unusual, so of course it has a story behind it. In the last chapter I shared about the accident my mom had in 1983. When she had the accident she was carrying a baby boy inside her womb; the baby was me! She had carried me for seven months and two weeks.

CHAPTER 2: Why The Name Live?

When the rescue team came, Mom had already lost consciousness, because she saw the lioness taking Placide, my elder brother. They took her to a nearby hospital that very night. My father continued home to the city of Kigali, where he met some of his friends in the morning and told them the tragedy of the accident and about his pregnant wife left dying on the bed of an unequipped hospital far in the east! There was no time to waste! Something had to be done as quickly as possible to save the life of his precious wife and hopefully that of their expected child.

It was good that my father had friends who are friends indeed. Among them was Emmanuel, who immediately jumped in his van and had all the seats removed so that a mattress could be placed inside. All this was done in a matter of minutes, and they headed back to the east at the hospital of Gahini where they found my father's friend, Bosco, who had stayed there to watch my mom. She really needed specialized doctors and a well-equipped hospital to treat her not only for her injuries but because of her pregnancy. Soon my father and his friends were on their way with Mom to the Central Hospital of Kigali in the city of Rwanda.

They reached the hospital in four hours and took my mother to the ICU, where she remained in an unconscious state for a couple of days. The doctors at this hospital had no knowledge of what to do so as to save my mother's life or mine, but papers and other identification documents were needed in order for her to be transferred to Europe for further treatment. With the help of my father's friend, Colonel Aloys, who was also the Minister and Secretary of State at the time, a transfer was issued in four days after the accident—an exceptionally quick amount of time! Travel arrangements were done and my mom was transferred to a hospital in the city of Brussels, in the country of Belgium.

At Burgman Hospital there were well-trained teams of nurses and doctors who were specialized and had access to more medical facilities and equipment to handle a case of this kind. To my father's surprise, they said that nothing could be done to save his wife or her unborn child. The only option they had was to abort me and save Mom; they gave me not even the smallest chance of survival.

Guess what? Doctors know much medically but little about God's plan. They can treat but not heal. Only one who shed His blood and paid the price for our healing as well as our eternal life can heal and save us. He is the miracle maker, the Savior of sinners, King of kings; Christ Jesus is His name.

In cases like this, where so small a chance has been given to an unborn child, the only option that fits to balance the equation is for men to say, "Do whatever you can and save my wife!" So, that is what my father said. The team of nurses and doctors decided to abort me, the unborn child, and they fixed a day for the operation.

Wow! Eh! Eh! This is the part I like, the reason for my name Live. As you can tell at this point there was no chance to turn this operation down unless by divine intervention! When they fixed the day nothing seemed able to change it, but God's last say for one life changed everything they had planned!

I know you really want to know what happened! All right, here is the miracle story. On the day scheduled for the operation, the doctor in charge didn't come! That's just the beginning of the rest of this birth miracle. So the operation was to be rescheduled. But on that same day, a pastor who often visited diseased persons in the hospital came to see my mother. She was hooked to a machine that helped her to breathe, and was held tight on the bed. Seeing this, the pastor closed his eyes

CHAPTER 2: Why The Name Live?

and bowed his head to pray. He got a vision and in that vision he saw two birds seated on the window of that room; one of them flew away leaving one behind. Later, the other bird flew away, and when they both returned they brought another bird with them, small and tiny. They stayed for a while on the window ledge. That was the end of his vision!

After the prayer, he shared the vision with mom's caretaker and gave the interpretation. The two birds were my parents, and the one who flew away signified my dad, in the way that he would leave for another wife because of my mom's illness. The one that later flew away signified my mom, as she was lying there sick, but that she would recover and give birth to a healthy baby boy, and that she would again live with her husband (my father).

Not only were there two birds sitting on the window later on that day, but everything the pastor stated in his interpretation happened at a future date.

Praise the Lord Christ Jesus, wow, isn't it wonderful? Just take a time to think about it; what would cause anybody to disagree that this was really God's miracle, that this man saw a vision of things that hadn't yet happened? Even before the pastor left the building, Mom was back to consciousness, and they told her all about his vision. She just wanted to hear it herself, so they searched for the pastor, and he came back. A lot of rejoicing was going on in that room as they celebrated that miracle. The pastor explained the vision to Mom, and also told her that God would grant her whatever she asked of Him at that time. The condition was that among the four requests she had to ask of God, three must be related to or concerned the unborn baby boy and one was for herself.

I just can't comprehend the faith these people had in God. Anyway, faith works, I know that for sure. And you know what's so funny? My mother never was upset that my father was going to leave her.

Mom's prayer on that day impacted the rest of my life, even though the prayer was made before my birth. This is what she asked God to do for her and me. First, she wanted to see me grown up. Then she asked that I would be a servant of God, that I would live long, and that I would have both knowledge and wisdom. Well, did God grant her prayer request? Yes, He did. Mom died when I was twenty, and I was serving God. I'm still acquiring knowledge, and I seek after wisdom by living what the Bible says in Job 28:28.

Miraculously born. Yes! I was. Mom and the pastor never saw each other again, but their interaction affected the rest of my life. When the nurses came to tell my mom what had been planned, immediately she refused to let them abort me and told them to do their best to save both of us, or to take her life to save mine. Oh, what a wonderful mother. I'm glad she didn't accept their idea as some of today's mothers would! If she had, you wouldn't be reading this book. There would be no Live Wesige.

It seems to be evident that I was given a chance to live, so there would be a miracle story to tell.

Another specialist was hired to handle my mother's case. He suggested that they create an incubator with same temperatures as those in the womb, and the next step was to take me out from the womb to the incubator. By now, I was eight months and few days, but still they gave me little chance of living. But when the operation was done, a healthy though premature baby boy was saved and secured in the incubator.

CHAPTER 2: Why The Name Live?

Hallelujah, God proved the words of the pastor and the vision to be really from Him.

Evidently this was a birth miracle, and that is the reason my name Live, as to live or to be alive, was given to me. Wesige is an African name that means believe, so my father gave me that name to tell my mom and me to believe and live. Like I told you, the parents are the first message senders to their child, as he or she develops self-concept and personality. I'm trying to live the message that my name carries and pass it on to others: believe and live.

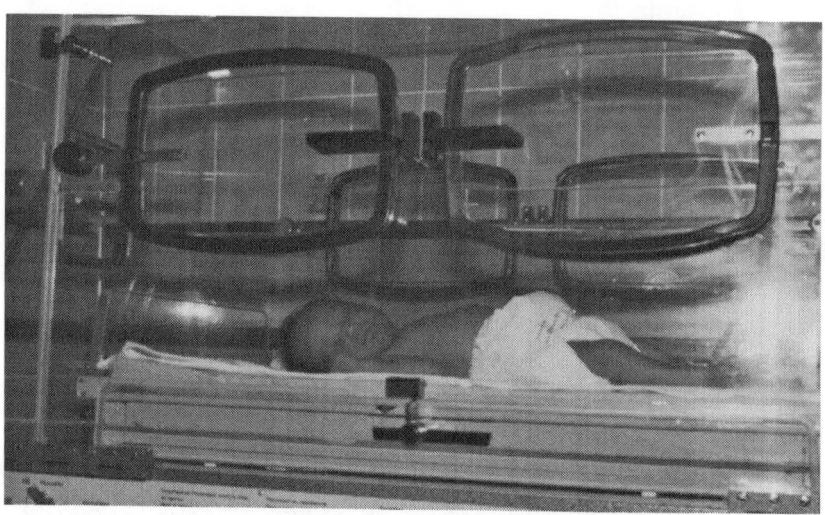

This is me in the incubator few days after my birth in 1983

THROUGH IT ALL: The Choice is Rejoice

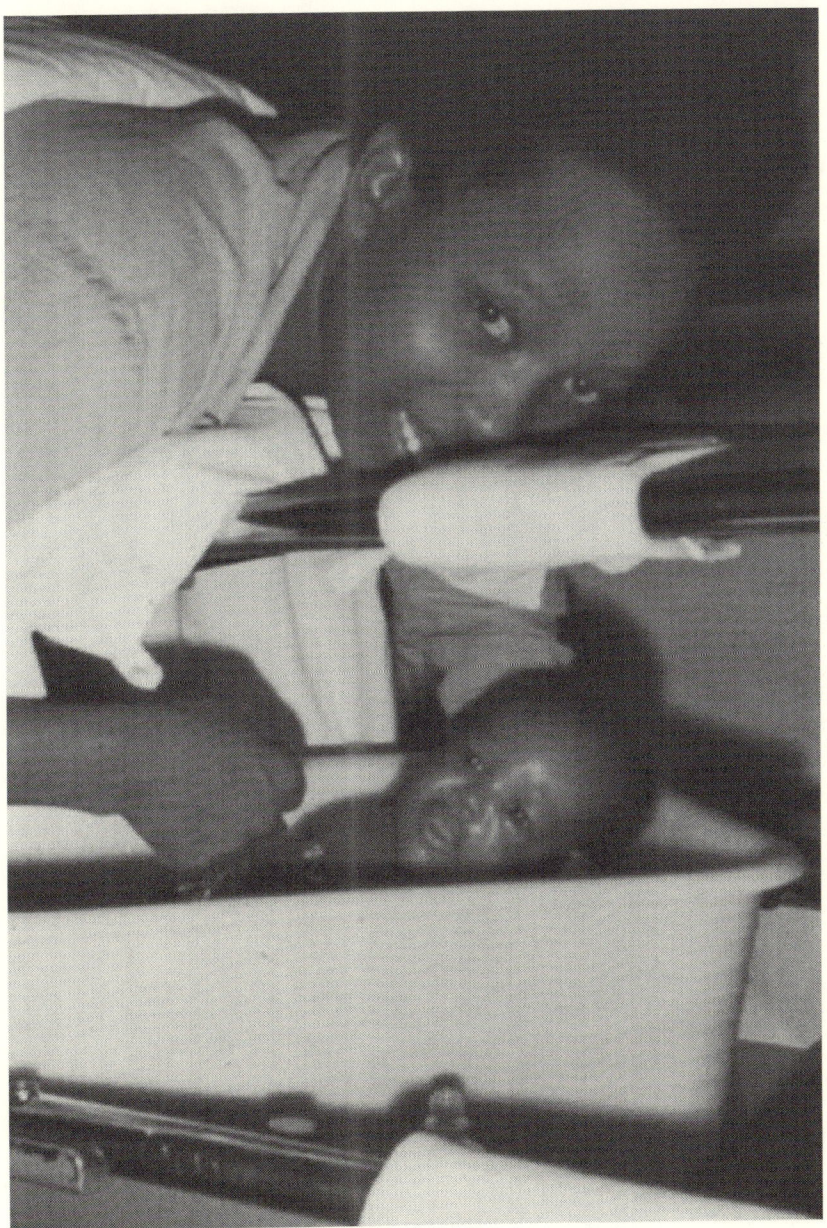

My mother giving me a bath at the hospital in Belgium

CHAPTER 2: Why The Name Live?

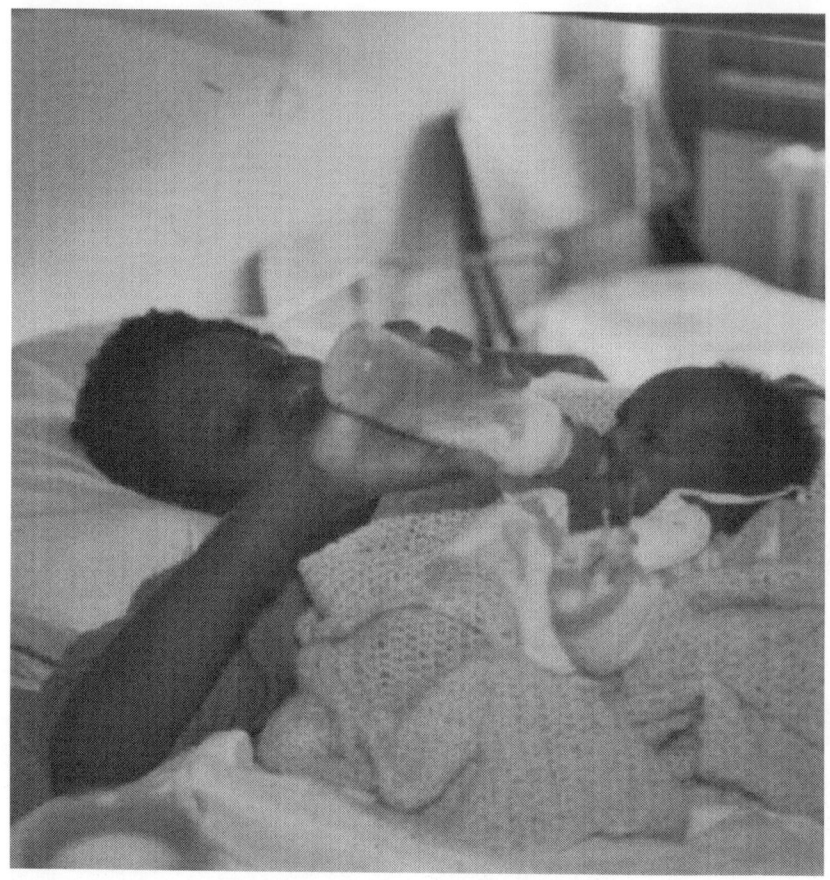

My mother bottle feeding me

THROUGH IT ALL: The Choice is Rejoice

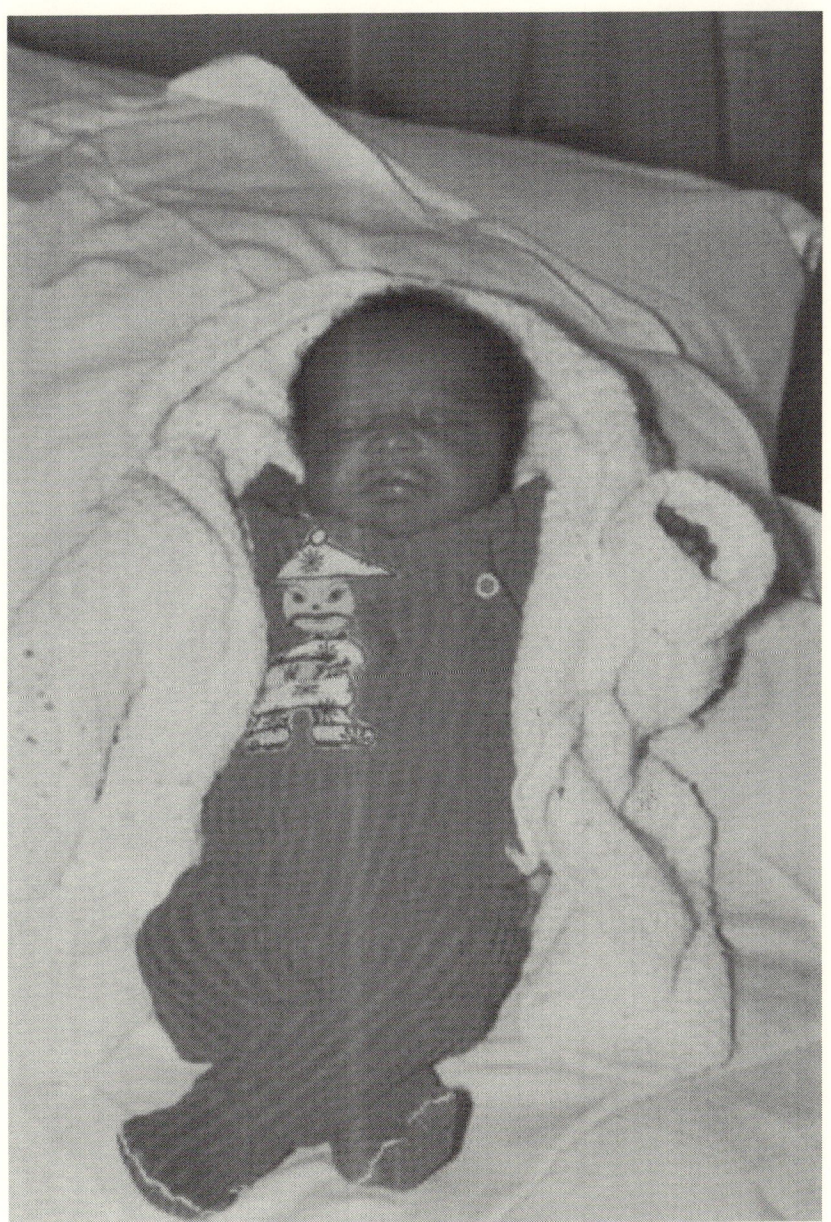

The day I was sent in Rwanda two weeks after my birth

CHAPTER 2: Why The Name Live?

THROUGH IT ALL: The Choice is Rejoice

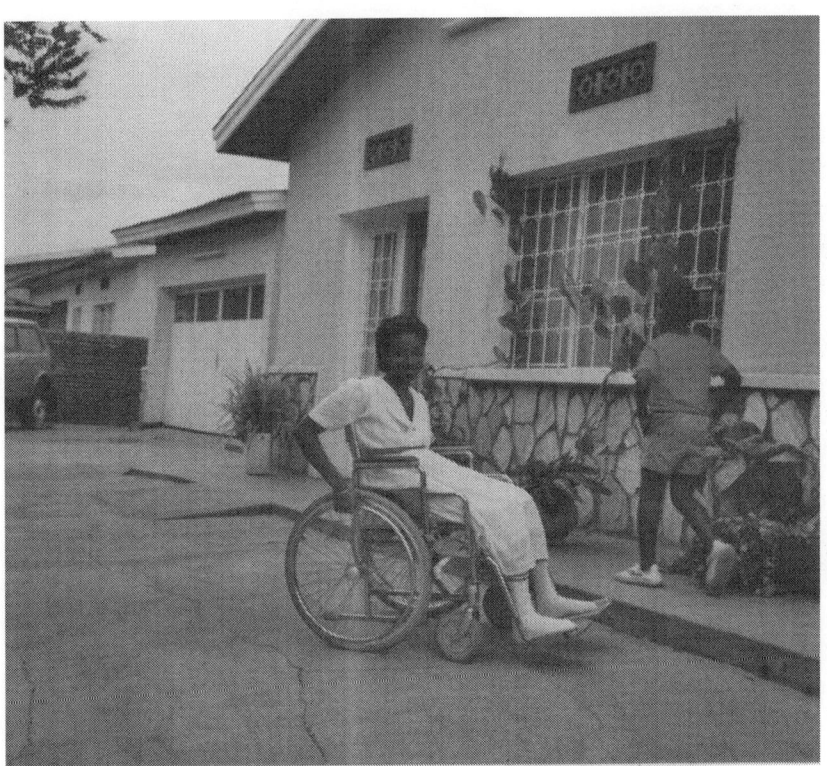

Mom and I in front of our houses in Kigali, she had been assigned to a wheelchair since 1983 to 2004 when she died.

CHAPTER 3
My Aunt, My Stepmother

Chapter 3: My Aunt, My Stepmother

Sadly, the term stepmother is almost unheard of unless "wicked" is attached to the front of it. While mothers are thought to be loving and kind, what is it about stepmothers that gives them an immediate negative connotation? Are some women born with the word "wicked stepmother" stamped on their foreheads, a form of predestination, or does one become a "wicked stepmother" as a learned response that enables one to cope with a family situation? Like many other things in life, only those who have the actual experiences are truly qualified to define them. All in all, a stepmother is defined as the wife of one's father, married to him by a subsequent marriage, not one's natural mother.

In my family the case was similar to many others. The only difference is that my stepmother was my mother's sibling. First, they shared the same parent, same discipline, you name it; they shared most everything in their lifetime, as well as the same husband. My mom was the eldest and the first wife. Just as the pastor God used to pray for my mom at the hospital in Brussels saw in his vision, my father walked away from my mother and married another wife.

A few days after my birth in November of 1983, the doctors suggested that it would be better to send me home and have my mom stay for further treatment. She wasn't able to take care of her baby boy because she was still held tight in the machines that they used to keep her from moving her back because she had seriously broken her spine during the accident.

Arrangements were made to take me home, and on the date that I was supposed to be born, I was actually in the hands of Sister Marie Michelle, a Belgian native who lived and still lives in Rwanda. She had accepted the responsibility of

CHAPTER 3: My Aunt, My Stepmother

delivering me to my father in Kigali. I met her couple of times while growing up, because she even helped my mom and me after the 1994 Rwandan genocide.

I don't remember this, of course, but I was told that upon my arrival at the airport there were a large number of family and friends who had accompanied my father to receive the miracle baby boy. There were moments of joy and celebration over what God had done to save my life and my mother's using the brains and skills of the doctors. Even though she remained in the hospital, at least there was more hope of her being healed than there had been of me living! Among the friends who came were Bosco and Emmanuel, who had helped take Mom to the hospital after the accident.

Anyway, my father being as busy he was with government work and politics was now a single man with two children. My elder brother Placide and I, the little premature born boy, made it very hard on him. He couldn't manage the role of a busy politician and that of a mother at the same time. So he brought my aunt, my mother's sister, into our home to be our caretaker. It meant he would not be so overwhelmed with responsibility.

But what happened was not so good. My father ended up having a love relationship with my mother's younger sister, whom he had only asked to help with the children. She got pregnant while her elder sister was still hospitalized, and it was due to this pregnancy that her love relationship with my father grew so rapidly. When my mom was discharged from the hospital to come home, she was terribly shocked to find out that she had been replaced by her own sister!

This created tremendous strife in the house. First of all, Mom was disappointed by the fact that she would no longer be able to walk; she had been assigned to live the rest of her life in a wheelchair due to paralysis of both her legs. Secondly, she was disappointed that the man of her dreams was cheating on her with her own sister! This was very sad.

My mother left and went to live with her parents, and sued for divorce. She was turned down and wasn't able to get a divorce, because Dad had been supported by his father-in-law. Then family members and friends gathered to discuss this issue. My father's defense mechanism, or excuse, was that he had done it in order to avoid a strange woman in the life of his first wife and boys. Was this a good defense? Yes, it was, even though he didn't wait to discuss it with my mom—and that was his first mistake. Secondly, he had sexually sinned against God outside of marriage! To me there was no excuse for that, but I was young anyway, so my vote wasn't of any help or even considered.

After the hearing, the family members and friends voted my father's rights to marry both my Mother and her sister. After all, they proclaimed, my mom could still play the role of a mother and wife in the house to a limit, and that's why she needed a helper! It's so sad that educated people like those family members and friends voted for polygamy, disregarding the Bible while confessing to be Christians.

My father, with the rights to polygamy, threw a big feast to welcome Mom back from her parents and also to pay the dowry for her sister. Whether they liked it or not, now these sisters had to share a husband and live in the same house. This made my aunt into my stepmother! Like I said earlier, to become a stepmother one must become a bride; and aren't brides, like mothers, usually associated with positive images? Yet if upon becoming a bride a woman also becomes a stepmother, it's amazing how fast that image can be disposed of and replaced

CHAPTER 3: My Aunt, My Stepmother

with another if she becomes a wicked stepmother, who mistreats her step children, instead of equally treating them as her own.

In our home I must say that it wasn't easy because there were, predictably, always disagreements between the two siblings sharing the same responsibility in the same house. It turned out to be worse than they expected, though, because they became really fierce rivals. Hence, hatred and jealousy were in our home. This affected my life because I didn't know to whom to relate as my mom. I later came to realize how much hate my stepmother had towards us and towards her own sister! She took total control of the household, instructing us what to do and what not to do. In addition to the do and don't regulations, orders were given our house maidens to not ever cook breakfast or wash clothes for my brother, my mom, or myself. She could get away with this because my father was not around; he had been imprisoned during this time for marrying two Tutsi wives. This was during the beginning of the 1990 war in Rwanda.

One day I was so sick that I couldn't go to school. I told my mom, who told me to tell my stepmom to take me to the hospital. What a disaster! My stepmom yelled at me and said that she had no time. She left me crying. When I went to knock at my mother's room she told me that she couldn't get up. Later my mom asked her sister, my stepmother, to take me; she said she would, but she never did! All she did was take me into my room, lock me there, and tell me to wait. I could cry, but our house was too big for Mom to hear me, and the maiden came to silence me through the window. I spent three days sick and nobody even cared.

My mom was in terrible pain at that time and didn't move from her bed for three days. Finally when she managed to get up, she came to see me. She called one of our house drivers, who took me to the hospital. I had a terrible case of malaria, a number one killer disease in Africa if not treated. I thank God that once again He saved me. This incident created even more tension and strife at this already difficult time.

There were other cruel things that I will not mention at this time. But growing up like that brought me to the understanding that God's love is unconditional, because whenever I tried to rebel against my stepmother, Mom, being a Christian, always told me that I wouldn't inherit the kingdom of God. Instead she told me to always pray for my stepmother to change even though she didn't love us.

My uncles who lived with us tried to calm the situation. With the order of my dad they fired the house maidens and brought in others who were given strict orders to be respectful to my mom and take care of us as well as they did our stepmom. We began to eat meals together, but then my stepmom tried to bring in poison to kill my mom—thankfully to no avail. There was much rivalry and strife!

When my father was released from the prison in 1990, he decided to sell that big house and buy two different houses so he could settle the tension between the two siblings. Well, he did sell the house, but again he made the same mistake of not hearing my mom's opinion. The money they were supposed to use to buy other houses was used to rent a two-story house where we stayed. This house was not conducive for my handicapped mom, so it was hard on her. The steps made it difficult for her to get out of the house if there was no one to help. Nevertheless; she kept her faith in and love for God.

During this time my mom sent me everywhere for anything she needed, but that only lasted for a couple of months until

CHAPTER 3: My Aunt, My Stepmother

she decided to move. One day everyone but Mom went to a wedding party, and later that evening when we came home she had already packed all her belongings and left. Now it was just my stepmom in that house. I felt abandoned knowing that my mother would no longer be there for me. I wondered where she was and how she was doing, although I was confused whether I should even ask if anybody knew where she was. Deep inside I was afraid, not knowing how my stepmother would treat Placide and me in the absence of our mother. To my surprise, she treated us differently once our mother was gone.

She started having problems with my dad because he was going through financial difficulties; there was political instability in the country, and he lost his office position due to his refusal to join the political party that was ruling then. Also, his gold business partner had stolen their investments, so we had to move to one of the unfinished houses to live there. My stepmom's health started declining and my stepsister was found to have HIV. Also my stepmom found out that Dad was having a love affair with a rich widow who she'd thought was their friend. She went to apologize to my mom after realizing that all her wickedness was very vain.

My aunt/stepmother died in the genocide along with another sister, and today nobody knows where they are buried. A sad ending for them, but my mom came back home. Remember the vision of the pastor in the hospital room about the two birds getting together again?

Read Proverbs 25:21-22 and Romans 12:19-21. Stop hating your enemy, overcome evil with good, and forgive whatever happens. Through it all we live to forgive. It is God's to repay and avenge.

THROUGH IT ALL: The Choice is Rejoice

Upper low left to right my dad Denys Zigama, mom Caritas Mukandekezi, step-mom Alphonsine Mukakirezi, bottom low left to right Jean-Pierre, my elder brother Placide Mizero, Live Wesige, my step brothers Denys Mubabo, Fiable Nibo and Sandrine Ingabire our cousin sister.

CHAPTER 4
My Innocence Abused

Chapter 4: My Innocence Abused

Child abuse can be physical, sexual, or emotional maltreatment or neglect by parents, guardians, or others responsible for a child's welfare. Physical abuse is characterized by physical injury, usually inflicted as the result of a beating or inappropriately harsh discipline. Sexual abuse of a child includes a wide range of actions between a child and an adult or older child. Often these involve body contact, but not always, and can encompass molestation, incest, rape, prostitution, or use of a child for pornographic purposes. Both physical and sexual abuse usually involve a severe form of emotional abuse as well. And some of this happened to me in different stages from the ages of seven to thirteen.

Most sexual abusers know the child they abuse, about one third of abusers are related to the child, and most abusers are men. In my case I was abused by both females and males. Child abuse has been reported up to eighty thousand times a year, but the number of unreported instances is estimated to be far greater, because the children are afraid to tell anyone what has happened.

Growing up in a family like I did, where we had two different people to call Mom, it was easy to be abused physically and emotionally because of the fighting between my mother and stepmother due to the fact that my stepmother was jealous.

I'm reminded of a day in early 1990, when I was about seven years old. A female visitor had come to our house urgently looking for one of our uncles, who had lived with us but later moved to live by himself. My father wasn't home, my mother couldn't walk, and I was the only child who knew where this uncle lived, so my mother asked me to take the visitor to see him.

CHAPTER 4: My Innocence Abused

At the time there were no cell phones in my country; the only way of communication was by landline telephones and the post office, and my uncle had none of these because he had just moved back from China. This visitor claimed to be my uncle's girlfriend, even though she didn't know that my uncle had moved.

Even though at my house children were supposed to be at home by six p.m. and it was already early evening, I think Mom allowed me to go because it was during the holidays and I had nothing to do. So with her permission I took this girl to where my uncle lived. I was excited because whenever I went to my uncle's house I was treated like a king. He gave me candy, cakes, and other sweet things to eat—not that we didn't have them home, but I liked it when it was from elsewhere. Anyway, when we reached my uncle's residence we knocked on the door and his house domestic came to open it, saying that uncle wasn't home yet.

I turned to go back home but the girl told me to stay and gave the domestic some money to buy milk, cakes, and candy. While we waited for him to return she told me different stories. When the domestic came back I ate the cake and drank the milk and I was full and sleepy. The girl told me to go to sleep and that when my uncle came home they would wake me up and take me home.

Around nine p.m. in the evening I awoke, immediately scared because I knew that I had violated the laws that governed children at home! I started to cry and my uncle, who had come home, asked what I was upset about. He told me that it was okay that I wasn't home, and he and his girlfriend and I started watching a video.

THROUGH IT ALL: The Choice is Rejoice

Soon after we heard someone knocking at the door. I felt certain it was someone coming for me. Sure enough, it was our domestic boy, whom they had sent to bring me back home. He said my father wanted to see me, so uncle didn't came with me. On the inside I was so scared about what would happen to me because I feared my father most, and I knew he didn't like us being in other homes, especially during the evenings!

At this time we had a very big compound fenced with brick walls and a big gate so nobody could see in from the outside, nor could anyone could enter unless the watchman allowed it. When we reached home we knocked to get in, and the watchman said that Dad had commanded them not to allow me inside but just to tell him when I arrived. They allowed our domestic in, leaving me behind.

Immediately I knew I was in trouble. I couldn't go back to my uncle's house, and I was so afraid of the dark. There was nothing else I could but knock hard, and I did; but the watchman refused to open the gate. I kept on loud enough that my dad heard it. But all he did was come out and ask me to leave his gate alone!

I started crying. "Let me in, Dad, please! Please don't leave me out here!" But he left. I was so angry that I picked up a stone and beat the gate even more loudly with it, demanding, "Open for me now!" Did he open? Did he care? No! Not at all, and in fear and desperation I sat there behind the gate crying. All of sudden, the watchman told me to run because my father was coming; he was angry and had a padlock in his hands. I said to him that I didn't care what my dad would do; I just needed to get in.

Oh, that was a bad night, I'm telling you! As soon as I finished talking to the watchman, Dad opened the gate and

CHAPTER 4: My Innocence Abused

struck me in the head with that padlock. Before I knew what was happening to me I was on the ground being harshly beaten; he kicked me in every part he could reach. I got up from the ground and ran towards the backyard, where I ran into my mom, who had been awakened by my noisy cries for help. I fell right next to her wheelchair, and she reached out and pulled me up with her hand. She asked what happened, but before I could explain there my father was with a squeegee. He began to beat me with it.

Mom tried to stop him, saying, "Stop it, don't kill my son!" My dad's response was, "No, he is my son, too, and I don't need rebels in my house." He kept on beating me and I continued to scream. Mom was also shouting at him to stop. Finally I jumped around my mom's wheelchair and she grabbed the squeegee to stop him. He pulled it back and tried to hit me again, but I dodged. Thankfully it missed Mom's hand, hitting the wheelchair handle instead.

After that Dad went inside, leaving Mom and me at the back door of the house. I was in terrible pain and my head was swollen from the blow of the padlock. That is only one of the many times I was physically abused with harsh discipline.

At this same age, I was sexually abused by a relative of my mother's who lived at our home. She attended the same school we did but had just completed her last year of primary and was on vacation, waiting for the results to be announced so she could go to high school. I had just graduated from kindergarten, joining the first year of primary!

One day this girl asked me to sleep on her bed for the night. I didn't know that anything wrong would happen; as innocent as I was I even told my mom that I was going to sleep with this girl, and so she let me! But later in the night the girl sexually

THROUGH IT ALL: The Choice is Rejoice

abused me and threatened to kill me if I ever told anyone about it. In fear of the death threat, I never told anyone, and she did this twice. Later, my stepmom found her sleeping with one of our domestic boys, so immediately she was sent back to her home.

I had another experience with sexual abuse at the age of nine. We were not supposed to watch TV or videos before six p.m., because we were accustomed to sleeping in our bedrooms every day after lunch if we didn't have classes to attend. Our neighbor's children had a movie they wanted to watch with us. We couldn't go over to their house, so they jumped the brick fence and came to our home, where we all sat together in the living room. No one else was home and at this time my mother had moved out to live by herself, as she was tired of being maltreated by both our dad and her sister. Dad and my stepmom had gone to their respective jobs, and we were home all by ourselves besides the domestics, who also wanted to watch the movie.

Unexpectedly, Dad came home to pick up something he had forgotten. When he came in, he found us seated in the living room watching a video. He had no idea where the video had come from, and in addition we weren't even supposed to be awake at the time. Finally, we had brought almost every child in the neighborhood into the house to watch with us. Oh, that was it. No excuses allowed! My elder brother Placide was in the most trouble; they held him responsible for everything, but with no exception we were all sent into the village to stay with our grandmother, where we would live for the rest of the holidays.

We didn't like going to the village. First of all, it meant no more movies and not as much fun as we had in the city, and besides, the comfort itself wasn't the same! For the first three

CHAPTER 4: My Innocence Abused

days it wasn't fun, but we adjusted because you know how grandmothers are to their grandsons; things were more and better! We enjoyed the farm life; seeing cattle, sheep, and goats was something else for a child like me who had been raised to always stay in the perimeter of the brick walls that fenced our compound! Actually, it was then that I saw a cow for the first time.

But at grandmother's house they assigned a domestic girl to take care of us. At first we thought this was wonderful, but this girl became my next abuser for three weeks. It all started after the attack by thieves, who broke into Grandma's house and robbed her of every valuable asset she owned. The thieves brutally attacked her, and my elder brother, and myself. This attack happened because they thought our father brought money every weekend when he came to visit.

Due to this attack, Placide slept in Grandma's bedroom and I was assigned to the domestic girl, who took advantage of that and forced me to have sex with her. She threatened me by saying that if anybody knew the things she was doing for me, *I* would be dead meat! Whenever I tried to talk to Grandma about it, I was told to shut my mouth and never say anything to anyone, just to accept whatever that domestic did! Grandmom didn't want to lose her after the many years she had been there.

I started feeling betrayed, isolated, and hated; and from that time I began to fear all women. This went on for three weeks. I lost a lot of weight during this time, which I could relate to what my father had done when I was seven, as well as to what my mother's cousin's sister had done. And now the domestic! It was horrible and I couldn't stop crying. Every day I went to hide in the banana plantation next to Grandma's peanut ground so that I would see nobody. The weekend my dad came to take us back home in the city I was finally relieved of the heavy burden of being sexually abused every night for three weeks.

I wish I could say that was the last instance of child abuse that happened to me! But in 1997 when I turned thirteen years old, I passed the primary examination with high marks and proudly joined high school. This was after the Rwandan 1994 genocide; I will talk about more about that in the next chapter. For now I'll share what happened to me after the war.

At high school, there was a tall boy who played basketball and was also very talented in the arts. Because I also had the same abilities in arts and basketball, we became friends even though he was older than me. I thought he was just being nice to me because we had similar talents, but I was wrong.

I didn't realize this until one day he acted differently. It was during break time and he asked me if I could join him for a cup of tea, which I accepted without hesitating since we didn't get tea at boarding school, and I loved tea. So we went out to the shop, and he bought a cup of tea with very sweet donuts, which I hadn't eaten for quite a time! He seemed happy and I was happy, thinking what a wonderful person he was; he had even saved me from being harshly teased by the elder boys in the dormitory.

After the cup of tea we still had time before we went back in our classes, so he said he had something to show me. He took me some ways away from any stores or other people and then suddenly took hold of my shoulders and commanded me to remove my trousers. "Wait a minute!" I screamed. "You are not going to do anything to me!" But before I knew it I was on the ground and he was holding a sharp knife over my neck. He said if I didn't remove my trousers and allow him to molest me he was going to kill me. In Africa it is more easily done

CHAPTER 4: My Innocence Abused

than said; someone could kill you and it would take eternity to discover the criminal. With this in mind I knew I couldn't get free unless I did as I was commanded.

I was a freshman and this boy was in his third level of high school. He molested me continuously from that time into my second year. At this time my school performance was declining and I couldn't talk to anyone about it. Finally I decided to drop out of high school; I stopped doing anything that would cause me to be with other people. That was the only way I found to get free from the evil in that boy.

I'm going to share one last part of this sad story! I was between the ages of fourteen and sixteen. I came home one night after many nights away from home, because I had rebelled against my parents, who wanted to make me go back to school. That night when I came home I ate but didn't go to see my mom, who was already sleeping. My dad wasn't home yet, but when he returned one of my stepbrothers told him that I was back. He didn't bother to ask where I had been or what had happened to me but went to his room and came back with a wired stick, which he kept for unknown reasons.

I hid myself under the bed but again my stepbrother told him where I was, so he pulled me out and started kicking and boxing me. Finally commanded me to lie down. He brought all four of my brothers into the living room where I lay tied with a loop on my legs. He told each of them to whip me five times with no mercy, and anyone who showed mercy would share portion of my punishment! Definitely no one needs to be punished for something he didn't do, so all four of them whipped me, after he took the time to give me a real slave-like beating.

I begged him to forgive me, promising that I wouldn't do it again; I even promised to go back to school. My mother heard me being whipped and crying out for help, but she couldn't get up so she called my brothers into her room and told them that if anything bad happened to me both them and my dad would be in so much trouble, because she would call the police to take them into prison. Once again she saved me from my father's harsh discipline. So Dad, feeling guilty that he hadn't even asked what had happened to me, commanded me to sleep in his bedroom; he had a different bedroom from my mom's.

In the middle of the night he told me how much he loved me and how sorry he was, but that very night he sexually molested me. The next day he got up and left early in the morning for the province where he worked. He left me a note on his bedroom dresser: *Remember, I have a gun and I can easily put you in jail, so don't ever try to tell anybody.*

When sexual abuse has occurred, a child develops a variety of distressing feelings, thoughts, and behaviors. Sexually abused children may develop the following:

- Unusual interest in or avoidance of all things of a sexual nature.
- Sleep problems and nightmares.
- Refusal to go to school.
- Depression or withdrawal from friends or family.
- Delinquency or conduct problems.
- Secretiveness, unusual aggressiveness, or suicidal thoughts.
- Fear that there is something wrong with their genital areas.

CHAPTER 4: My Innocence Abused

All these things happened to me as result of my abuse, and if it weren't for God's unfailing love I might already be dead. Instead I'm here to tell you, that *through it all*, live to forgive and you can still smile! Learn to avoid the regrets of the past, the boredom of the present, and the fear of the future. I will explain more about this in one of the chapters ahead. But If you are struggling in these areas, it may be because you have been abused, and I recommend God as the ultimate answer. Hopefully some of the following chapters of this book will also help you, as you read how God helped me to overcome.

CHAPTER 4: My Innocence Abused

Me at the age 7 and 9 when I was sexually abused

CHAPTER 5
Over a Million Lost Their Lives

Chapter 5: Over a Million Lost Their Lives

In this chapter I will be talking about a genocide that happened in Rwanda, my mother country. Rwanda is one of the smallest countries in central Africa, with a population between eight and nine million people, and is comprised of three ethnic groups, the Hutus, Tutsis, and a less known ethnic group, the Abatwa. Although the Hutus account for 90 percent of the population, in the past the Tutsi minority was considered the aristocracy of Rwanda and dominated Hutu peasants for decades, especially while Rwanda was under Belgian colonial rule. The three ethnic groups are actually very similar; they speak the same language, inhabit the same areas, and follow the same traditions with the exception of the Abatwa. But when the Belgians colonists arrived in 1916, they saw the three groups as distinct entities and even produced identity cards classifying people according to their ethnicity.

Ethnic tension in Rwanda is nothing new; there have always been tribal disagreements, but animosity has grown substantially since the colonial period. Following independence from Belgium in 1962, the Hutus seized power and reversed the roles, oppressing the Tutsis through systematic discrimination and acts of violence. As a result, over two hundred thousand Tutsis fled to neighboring countries and formed a rebel guerrilla army, the Rwandan Patriotic Front (RPF).

In 1990, this rebel army invaded Rwanda and forced President Juvenal Habyarimana into signing an accord that mandated that Rwandans would share power. Ethnic tensions in Rwanda were significantly heightened and in October 1990 my father was put in jail for hiding his friend (Bosco), whom the government army wanted to kill, just because of how he was created! My father was also considered a traitor because he was married to a different tribe than the one in power. By

CHAPTER 5: Over a Million Lost Their Lives

1993 the tension had gone far beyond control, and a United Nations peacekeeping force of 2,500 multinational soldiers was dispatched to Rwanda to preserve the fragile cease-fire between the government and the rebel guerrilla army. Peace was continuously threatened by extremists who were violently opposed to sharing any power. Thus, ethnic riots broke out in Kigali, Rwanda.

Rwanda's genocide occurred between April and June 1994; an estimated one million Rwandans were killed and killings did not subside until three months later. As many as ten thousand were killed each day! This became Africa's largest genocide in modern times.

The genocide was sparked by the death of the president Juvenal Habyarimana, when his plane was shot down above Kigali airport on April 6, 1994. Within hours after the death of the president, Rwanda plunged into political violence as extremists began targeting prominent opposition figures, and a campaign of killings and violence spread throughout the countryside as militias armed with machetes, clubs, axes, pickaxes, guns, and grenades began indiscriminately killing innocent civilians. People were pulled from their cars and their identification cards were checked; these tribal cards now meant the difference between life and death. The state radio encouraged the killings by broadcasting hate propaganda nonstop and even pinpointing the location of the people in hiding. Killers were also aided by the professional class including journalists, doctors, and educators, along with unemployed youth and peasants who killed their neighbors just to steal their property.

Many people futilely took refuge in churches and mission compounds, which then became the scenes for some of the worst massacres. Hospitals also become targets as wounded survivors were sought out then killed. In some local villages militiamen forced family members to kill their relatives and friends or face death sentences themselves.

When all this happened, I was about ten years old! I am among many eyewitness survivors and still remember what I saw. There are many things that I will never forget, and I am willing to share some of great miracles that happened to me during in those horrible and terrifying dark days of my life.

As I have said, my family lived in Kigali, the capital city of Rwanda. Our house bordered the fence of the airport where the president's plane was shot down by a rocket. On the third day of violence, a group of armed militia broke into our house claiming that we were hiding enemies of the country and weapons, so they threw everything out of the house in search of these weapons and rebels. It worsened when the group found the identity card of my stepmother, who was from a targeted tribe. Also, my father had just come from a work mission in Italy and had a big, locked suitcase; nobody knew the code to open it. For those two reasons they told us to get out of the house, where they commanded everyone to lie down on our faces in the front yard. They said they were going to shoot all of us.

Well, God protected us. We were new in that neighborhood, and a neighbor we didn't even know came and stopped them. The next day they returned, but my father gave their chief leader a house with all the paperwork, which held them off a little longer. When the final attack came it was a mixture of soldiers and militia asking for money. They also took our stepmother and were going to cut her in pieces with machetes. They said they would then come back to burn us alive in the house! But when they reached the hole into which they threw

CHAPTER 5: Over a Million Lost Their Lives

the victims alive or dead, instead of killing my stepmother they let her come back home.

On April, 10th, 1994, the neighbor who had stopped the first group took us children to his home to hide us there. That night we went back to our house, packed everything possible, and left immediately. We didn't know where we were going, but our stepmom refused to come with us and stayed in the house. She was later killed along with my one and only sister, who was three years old.

As we fled, we reached a school called Ecole Technique de Kicukiro where we decided to hide together with other people we met along the way. The next morning the Belgian and French soldiers who guarded the school left. Within minutes the school was attacked by armed militia stoning to death those who were on the playground. They raped young girls and buried them alive. They burnt many of the people alive, cut others into pieces, and many of the victims were taken to a slaughter ground in Nyanza. As the number of people decreased, the survivors decided to gather together to find a way of escape. There was little hope, as we were surrounded by battle tanks. Most of the people in the classroom where I was lost their lives, including our family's domestic girl. By God's grace I survived by hiding underneath a woman's dead body. I lay under her skirt and pretended I, too, was dead.

Militiamen spent an entire day killing innocent people hiding at the school. When the sun set, I ran away through the bushes and spent the night outside. The next morning I woke up to the realization that I had spent the night next to a bundle of many dead bodies, most of them women and young girls. I traced my way back to the school to see if I could at least find my dad or anyone I knew. I found nobody! I became so worried and fearful that I joined a group of people going into one of the houses. On the way I saw a dog carrying the arm of a dead person! Dead bodies were all over the roads and flesh-eating birds surrounded those piles of dead people.

The group I was with was welcomed into the house, so I thought I now had a safe place to stay. Nobody seemed to care about my presence there; however, the owner came to me and asked me who I was and what I was doing in his compound. I answered him with honesty and told him everything about myself. He turned around and I heard him whisper to one of the other guys that I was a cockroach (the term they used to describe their targets). Hearing that, I knew that if I delayed to escape I would be dead meat. So slowly I turned and jumped the brick wall, falling outside the compound.

I thought that it was finished and I was safe, only to realize that a few meters from the compound was a roadblock where many people had been killed; in fact, three people got killed right in front of my eyes! One was pierced with a spear, the other one was cut by machetes, and the third one was shot with three bullets in his forehead after being beaten by clubs. The people who were killing them saw me jumping and called for me, but I ignored them and started running. Surely again God performed a miracle and saved me, preventing the evil from catching me; and He didn't allow any of the bullets to reach me! Hallelujah, praise the Lord.

Running away from those wicked people, I found my young stepbrothers. One of them was stuck in ditch and was crying for help, calling out our father's name. I stopped to pull him out of the ditch, and after a few more meters I saw the other one lodged under a fallen tree. We tried to lift up the big heavy tree and managed to pull him out, and then we continued running. As we ran I repeatedly asked them if any of them knew the whereabouts of Dad or Placide. They couldn't

CHAPTER 5: Over a Million Lost Their Lives

answer, as both of them were very young; one was five and the other four. I held their hands and kept on running, following the crowd of those fleeing from all the shooting.

There were many bombs hitting the ground all around us, and it was in the forest at Rebero Mountain that a woman who was holding the hands of her young son, with another child on her back and her husband was in front of them, had a bomb fall on her. My brothers and I were behind her; we lay down on the ground and a big, loud noise broke my ears for some time. My eyes were closed and I thought I was dead! But later I realized that I still could breathe, so I opened my eyes. When I did, there was mist of dust, and I saw half a hand on my arm; it was that lady's hand. Ooh, I will never forget that image of this family's small pieces of human flesh mixed with bones.

That was another salvation day! God had protected me again. My brothers were also still alive, so we closed our eyes and passed the bloody, heartbreaking image of that dead family and continued towards a small village that I could see from a distance. When we approached those houses, we stopped and slowly moved towards a bush near at the back of one of them. One of my young brothers told me that he was hungry, but I had no food, neither did I have any money on me. I didn't know what to do!

Let me testify about God's provision in such a way that you will definitely praise Him for His love and provision of our daily bread. When I found that I couldn't get my brothers any food, I remembered a story I had heard in Sunday school when Jesus fed over five thousand people from only five loaves of bread and two fish. With this in mind I began to pray and asked Jesus to give me food for myself and the kids, and at the end of my prayer even though I didn't know much about religion or anything about salvation, I was answered. I smelled the sweet aroma of pork meat, so I told my brothers to stay in the bush. I didn't know where I was going but I decided to follow the aroma. It was a choice between life and death.

On my way there I came across a dog that had a piece of a human flesh in its mouth, although I couldn't identify to which part of the body the flesh belonged! Still, I could see the human skin on that piece of flesh as the dog dug a hole to hide it. I scared it away. Then I continued towards the aroma and saw a group of people seated around a pot of fried pork meat. These people had machetes, clubs, and guns, but suddenly there was the sound of a bomb blast close by and all these people got inside the house. I ran to get the pot of pork meat. Ha! That's how I got the food. But one of them saw me stealing the pot and the whole group came searching in the bush to kill us.

Among the killers was a man who used to be the watchman at our house. He remembered me and even remembered that, when he had been stopped from working at our house, I gave him some money (less than a dollar) to use for transportation because my father denied paying him! But regardless of all the hurt my dad caused him, he chose to forgive and have compassion on us and stopped the killers from killings us. Then he took us in and ordered food for us. There I also met my cousin's brother. My cousin was the elder and he took us to an old woman who cared for us for three days.

After that the soldiers and militia at the roadblock behind this old woman's house saw me. They surrounded her house compound. One of them was a fine looking young man they had nicknamed Agaca, because he had killed many people. He came to tell the old lady that he wanted the cockroach that was hiding there in her house. The old lady told him that we were her grandchildren, but he knew she was lying so

CHAPTER 5: Over a Million Lost Their Lives

he insisted. She told him to search the house, and when he came inside, guess what? I was there seated in the living room drinking milk. I reached out to greet him, handed my milk to him, and told him that I knew he was going to kill me but that I wanted him to drink my milk before he did anything else!

At end of my depressed speech, he looked me in the eyes and asked who my father was. I explained my background. He asked me to think of how I would like to be killed, giving me options like being cut into pieces, shot in the head, and more. Once I answered his questions I could see his eyes fill with compassion, and he sat and drank my milk. Then he got up and left the house, instructing the rest of his troop to leave. Then he invited me over where he stayed! Hallelujah! God is good again; He protected my siblings and me.

The next day, when my dad passed through that roadblock, Agaca was there and inquired for my father's identity card. Then Agaca asked him if he knew where his children were. My father said he didn't know but thought they were dead, and Agaca said to him, "No, I know where they are; come with me." And he brought Dad to us.

My dad stayed with us for two days before he was escorted into the city, where he sent for us. We joined him, but later we evacuated from the city of Kigali and drove toward the north, when we reached a place called Nyundo. Our car was stopped and again they asked Dad for his identity card! They asked him the tribe of his wives, then pulled me out and tied me with my arms behind against on a tree. My dad negotiated and even showed them identification papers proving that he was my father. But they kept refusing and said to him that I wasn't his based on my physical appearance! So I deserved to die.

THROUGH IT ALL: The Choice is Rejoice

At this point I knew that my father's money couldn't save me nor could his influence, so I started praying inwardly, asking God to save me once again. Well, He did! A truck approached the roadblock; this truck was coming to pick up the soldiers to go elsewhere as reinforcement troops. The chief of the armed militia in that area and a senior soldier who also was the driver gave orders that everyone stationed at that roadblock had to join them. The soldiers left one of their men behind, and my dad got out of the car and paid this soldier to let me go. This man accepted the bribe and untied me. Then we continued to the city of Gisenyi, and that night we crossed the border and fled into exile in Zaire, present day Democratic Republic of Congo.

In July of 1994 a rebel guerrilla army movement captured Rwanda's capital city Kigali and the killings ended. But by then over a million people had lost their lives. At this particular time rebellious people began to avenge the lives of their family or friends and killed a huge number of other innocent people in the refugee camps in Byumba, Gikongoro, and even across the borders of the country.

God saved me and some of my family members, even though many of our relatives died. As a survivor I'm here to tell you that God kept me through it all and I can still smile. I give thanks to God, who saved me, and continually pray for those who lost their family and friends, as well as for you, the reader of this book: that you will find the true joy in life. "Let us not repay evil for evil, but always follow what brings peace and do good, showing kindness to everyone" (1 Thessalonians 5:15-18).

CHAPTER 5: Over a Million Lost Their Lives

Few months before the 1994 Rwandan Genocide, in this picture from upper left to right Live Wesige at the age of 10, step-mom Alphonsine Mukakirezi, Placide Mizero my elder brother, from bottom left to right Denys Mubabo, Mahoro Mahire peace and Nibo Fiable my step siblings. Both Alphonsine and Peace died in 1994.

CHAPTER 6
Survivor in Exile

Chapter 6 : Survivor in Exile

We got a chance to cross over to exile in Zaire, present day Democratic Republic of Congo, in the middle of June 1994. We (Dad, my stepbrothers, and me) had fled during the night, since we couldn't cross during daytime because militia and military soldiers were all around the border trying to stop and kill those who fled the country. We left the car at the other side of Gisenyi and walked across through difficulties.

When we arrived in Zaire, the Congolese soldiers were not sociable; they took away my dad's briefcase, searched it, and robbed him all the francs (Rwandan money) he had with him. They didn't even leave us a coin! On the top of that, my father was slapped and kicked, and they ordered us to leave. That was our entry to a series of trials in exile, the first experience as refugees.

Speaking of the slap, I'm reminded of the scripture that says to do for others whatever you want done to you (Matthew 7:12). Well, I think my father reaped what he sowed! It was routine to attend church services every Sunday, but he had stopped going; he only went on big Christian religious holidays. This was because in 1992 a refugee from the northern part of our country hit the side mirror of his new Peugeot 309 and broke it. This was unintentional; he was only playing with my younger stepbrother in the church parking lot when it happened. My father and I were in the service inside the church, and my young brother came in and whispered to my father that his side mirror was broken. He immediately told me to get up and go outside with him, and he asked who the boy was. The other children pinpointed that refugee boy, and my father slapped him, kicked him, and locked him in the trunk of the car. Then he came back and sat as a holy saint in the church till the end of service, and even drove to a restaurant, as was our

CHAPTER 6: Survivor in Exile

custom every Sunday. There he bragged about his evil deed, and I was so upset with him that I spoke to one of his friends, whom we met at the restaurant, and told him about the boy in the trunk. Through this man that boy was released, and my punishment was to walk home from the restaurant, which I happily accepted. But my father's time to reap came when we crossed the border and became refugees; the slap and kicks he delivered to that refugee boy at church he reaped in exile.

Like I said earlier, it was a series of trials for us as survivors in exile. First, because Dad had no money, we couldn't rent a house so we lived on streets; later we moved to live in a church, and it was at this church that I acquired a deadly disease called cholera due to malnutrition and poor sanitary conditions, mostly the water. We lived in the town of Goma on the shores of Lake Kivu in which many dead corpses were thrown during the mass killings in Rwanda. This water was polluted not only with dead bodies but also with all the waste products from the industries built around the lake in both countries, Rwanda and former Zaire.

It wasn't possible to get proper treatment, so the disease worsened on a daily basis. I became very dehydrated, losing water as well as blood, and my belly was kind of full all the time even though I had no appetite at all! One day in the evening after I had prepared rice for dinner and green vegetables, I felt like I was dying, so I went to sleep on a mat on the dusty floor of the church. After a while I got up to feed my young brothers who were with me at the time; my father always left early in the morning in search of a job, only to return drunk every evening; he never cared about anything. After I fed them it was time to sleep.

On that evening many refugees came to that church from Rwanda, among them a couple that were friends with my dad.

For the next few days the wife took care of us. I told her how I was losing a lot of blood and water, and she told me to lie down and then made me egg soup, which I failed to eat; my stomach was in terrible pain. That was the second night after this couple moved in to stay in the church with many other families; on the fourth day six people died of lack of proper treatments for cholera, which had been spread all around that village.

I grew skinnier daily, until my dad knew about my sickness and tried to get me medicine. But it was too late; the medicine was not affordable to us, so they made a drip of salt mixed with boiled water, and eggs to eat. This was my diet and medicine for some days. People were surprised by me because older people with stronger immune systems were killed in a matter of hours, but I pushed on for days.

Nevertheless, on the evening of the fifth day I got terribly weak and my father wasn't there; he had gone into a bar with his cousin's brother Fredrick and his friend Innocent, who lived with us at the church. I was left at the church with Innocent's wife Liberatta and my young brothers. As I became weaker and weaker I told them to lie me in the church on the mat. On the mat they helped to hold my arms stretched out with my legs straight to make a cross sign. In seconds my eyes were closed.

The next thing I saw was a very fine looking, tall man clothed in white robes. He had a syringe in his right hand. As I looked into his eyes with fear, he smiled and said to me, "Don't fear. He who sends me says you will serve Him." He asked me to turn around so he could give me a shot. This was absolutely ridiculous since I didn't know who had sent him, but in obedience I turned, and he gave me the injection.

CHAPTER 6: Survivor in Exile

When all this took place, in my mind I thought I was conscious of my surroundings. But, no, I wasn't! In fact, I was to be thrown along the roadside, just like they did to everybody that died in those days of despair, as refugees in Zaire. Little did I know that this was two hours after I'd fallen asleep, because they thought I was dead and they had nothing else to do with me.

My father had permitted this, and Fredrick his cousin and Innocent his friend had actually wrapped me in the mat on which I slept on and were carrying me. But when the big man I saw asked me to turn, I did in my sleep. They dropped me and ran, shouting, "He is alive!" Others were screaming as though they had seen a demon!

I knew nothing at all, but after the shot my strength was renewed and I was completely out pain. Hallelujah, God had miraculously healed me. I unwrapped myself from the mat, stood and picked it up, and started running behind those who were screaming and shouting. I had no idea that they were running away from me! Fredrick stopped and turned back, commanding me to stand still, which I did in obedience. He said, "You are dead!"

"Dead!" I answered back in surprise. "No! No! I am not dead, I'm alive. I just finished talking with a tall, fine looking man who wore white robes."

They laughed at me and said, "No! You are dead." They called my father to question me, and he asked me what my favorite nickname was. I told him with much confidence, and he didn't even wait to hear my answer because he was very excited to see his son back to from the dead. He hugged me and held my hands. I started telling everyone the whole story of the tall man and what he had said to me, but they didn't seem to believe me. Instead my dad told me not to mention it again and proceeded to say that everybody who was unconscious saw and heard unusual things, and that's what had happened to me!

Parents make such mistakes just because they are not willing to believe what their children say, or because they don't understand their children's experience of divine visitation. My father didn't believe in a divine visitation of God's angels; neither did he know much about miracles since he called them "good luck" or "chances"; he was just religious like most parents of this present age. He was convinced that I hadn't seen an angel. I remained silent about this divine healing by God's touch through an angel until the time I became born again and began to study God's Word. I realized the truth about the ministry of angels to men during a Bible class at Apostolique pour le Reveille au Rwanda, the first Pentecostal church I attended, where I was born again in 1999!

God is always faithful, even though we aren't. After my miraculous healing, life wasn't easy as it had been before in my country, but by all means we had to survive the situation. We moved from the church to live in an incomplete building in a place called Birere in Goma, where my dad and his friend rented a house. Then my father went to Bukavu to visit his brother, who had also fled the country. He spent a week there.

Back in Goma, Liberatta was giving me a hard time! She always sent me to the market and used me in all the home duties, even sending me to beg for money. One day, I went into a Congolese home to beg for water because I was thirsty, but instead of water they locked their gate. I couldn't get out and they released their dog, which attacked me. Praise God I was able to jump the fence, but the dog got hold of the shoe on my left foot! I had to walk all the way home barefooted,

CHAPTER 6: Survivor in Exile

crying, and the Congolese children were running behind me throwing stones at me. Luckily I met a man who stopped them and gave me a packet of biscuits, and I went back home.

After that week, when my dad returned, I explained everything that happened to me while he was gone. He took time to listen to me, and then he told me that he had already arranged a travel to Bukavu, where I would stay with my uncle Baptiste and his pregnant wife Theresa.

In Bukavu things were little bit better; to me it's just a reminder that what you sow is what you reap. From 1990–1993 there had been war in different parts of Rwanda, and there were many refugees who fled from the north to Kigali and some neighboring districts. These people always moved from house to house in search for food, clothes, and financial help. My mom loved to help them, so every Friday we had a group refugees at her work. It's for this reason that I always gave away some of what God had blessed me with; even though I was young I knew the principal of giving. Little did I know that my giving to refugees was actually planning ahead because the Bible promises that a generous man shall be made fat, enriched, and prosperous (Proverbs 11:25). I was preparing my way, because when I became a refugee, God made a way for me to be in exile but still live a better life than most refugees, who lived in tents and had little to eat. This was my harvest for treating with compassion all those refugees who passed by our house every Friday.

At the beginning, life in Bukavu was tough for me because I was learning a lot of new things that I wasn't used to doing, like washing dishes, washing my own clothes, cooking, and all the domestic work you can name. I didn't care that life was hard, since my uncle Jean Baptiste and his wife Theresa took good care of me. In a short period of time we moved from Bukavu to Kenya in eastern Africa. We took a flight, my first time in an airplane.

You see, it was as if we weren't refugees, another sign of God's blessing over my life; there is no other way to describe it. I mean, just imagine: a few days earlier I was lying dead without knowing what God had in store for me. Oh! God is so wonderful and He has plans of hope and future for every human soul that believes in His name (Proverbs 19:23).

On the way to Kenya we flew from Bukavu to Goma, where we stayed in hotel for a week. Somehow the airplane we were supposed to connect with from there to Nairobi had trouble getting there from Kinshasa, the capital city of former Zaire. Take a minute and think about this. I spent a week in the same city where I was previously going to be buried! Why did God bring me back there? I didn't figure it out at the time, but now I understand that it was to teach me and everybody else that the same place where you have spent time in failure and in problems, that is where God is going to teach you about His love for you, His provision, and His protection.

When the plane finally came we safely reached Kenya and stayed in hotel for two weeks. Later my uncle rented a house in western part of Nairobi. I couldn't speak English or Swahili, which are the main languages in Kenya, as they have many other tribal languages. It took me a few months to adjust to the surroundings, and then I went to learn English and Swahili at a Catholic school in Kayore. This was quite exciting because I met people from my own country and life seemed well. But within me I had a sense of isolation.

There was an older boy who attended the same language classes as I did even though he was older—and by the way, he wasn't the oldest; we even had old men and women in the

CHAPTER 6: Survivor in Exile

same class! Patrick and I developed a friendship that caused me a lot of trouble. First, he told me how many people he had killed in the genocide, and he threatened to kill me if I ever said anything about him to anybody! Then he started sending me to one of the girls who also attended that school but was in a different class, and she reported to the teacher that I was always coming after her and telling her silly words of love. Later Patrick attacked me with a knife and told me that I had to give him money, so in order to save my life I promised to pay him every week.

Where do you think I could get money? Of course, this meant I was going to steal it from my uncle, which I did. For the first couple of days I was successful, but later I was caught in the action. Betty, who was our neighbor, came to see my uncle's wife. Her husband and Uncle Baptiste were good old friends. My uncle wasn't home as he had gone to work. His friend had gone to Tanzania where he ran a business, so I knew for sure that nobody would catch me stealing in their apartment. I stole the house key from Betty and went downstairs to where they lived, slowly entered, and locked myself in. I started searching for money, little knowing that it was my last day of such bad behavior. Not only is it bad behavior but also it is sin (Exodus 20:15).

While I was in the middle of my search for money to steal, Betty's husband showed up; as usual he had a spare key. Oh! What bad luck for a thief! He opened the door and asked me what I was doing in his house. Before I could say a word he punched me, hit me, and kicked me; he really had seen that I was trying to steal their money. He took me by the pants and threw me out of his apartment. Then he closed the door to his house and took me upstairs to my uncle's apartment.

The two women looked at me and didn't say a word. When Uncle came home and was told that his nephew was the thief being hunted all over in this apartment building, he didn't wait for an explanation. He just asked me to lie down and then he whipped me, seriously. I promised that I wouldn't do it again.

I could have told them the cause, but when asked why I was stealing, I kept quiet. I feared Patrick's threats, so instead I developed friendship with Didier, a big boy at school, whom I always stayed near. He protected me from Patrick and that was the last I heard of him.

A few weeks later my uncle's firstborn, who was only a year and few months old and the only child they had at the time, died of malaria, which was discovered only few minutes before his death. It killed him because they had been treating him for a different disease; all this was a result of poorly trained medical professionals in Kenya. It was a grieving period in my life because this baby kept me busy while I wasn't at school, and I had more than enough fun with him; to me it was like losing not only a cousin but also a close friend. A few days later Theresa, his mom, got a job and went to work in the same place as my uncle. We moved and went to live in another part of Nairobi called Gong Hills.

In this new area we lived in a very rich community, so I stayed in the compound of the house at all times and knew nobody in the neighborhood. We lived within the compound of my uncle's employers, who were Chinese, and they enrolled me in a school far out of Nairobi, a Seventh Day Adventist boarding school. This was extremely far away from anything, close to Mount Kenya in Kirinyaga, and while the school hosted a few Rwandans studying there it was mostly Kenyans.

CHAPTER 6: Survivor in Exile

Oh! How things can change. I changed from being a thief and to becoming very legalistic about the Sabbath day. The hand of God was upon me at the time. I did well in class and was the third among the class of forty students. I performed well in science, music, arts and crafts, and even mathematics. School life was enjoyable and fun—until the second trimester when we returned from holidays. Everybody was happy and we had lots of stories about our holidays, but my mattress had been eaten and torn apart by rats, so I had a mattress with a very big hole that extended from the center to the edge of the right side. I couldn't easily communicate with my uncle, so I had to wait until the visiting day, which was only once a month—and he didn't come on the first visiting day. The second visiting day he sent someone in his place, and I gave that person a letter explaining what had happened with my mattress and that I needed another one.

Uncle delayed in bringing it, and all this time the other children mocked and laughed at me. During this time such offences were common to me; it was just another chapter of life where I had to receive whatever happened, since I was a refugee and was being accused of killing other people in my country—just because I was a Rwandan! Please understand that these students who called me genocidal knew nothing about what had happened; the fact that I was Rwandan simply meant I had to be a murderer.

I found comfort in passing my tests and exams and scoring higher grades than the Kenyans, who still made me feel rejected and hated by both humans and God. I couldn't understand why all this was happening to me. No sooner than this mental torture began than I realized that it was not only the students participating but even some teachers. I never forgot one particular teacher, who stole my art competition rewards along with twenty-five thousand Kenyan shillings, and placed the artwork on his own living room wall.

Since we were a religious school the students attended Sabbath services at school. We didn't eat on Saturday morning, and we wore a different kind of uniform on the Sabbath. This was all good, interesting, and fun, and it was from this school that I learned about God again. Certainly with the situation that I was going through I began seeking God for love and protection. He reminded me of the vision of the big man that I'd seen in Zaire, and how he miraculously healed me. I promised that I was going to serve God, and I really developed a deep sense of His love and presence.

Because of this I felt that I should share a thought or a teaching with the Sabbath school, and the idea was welcomed by our school chaplain, who insisted that I do it on Saturday during Sabbath service. I prepared myself to deliver my message. I stood to talk to the congregation of students and teachers about what I intended to share: it was about the ark that Noah built and how all different types of animals lived together in harmony and peace. I did mention cats and rats, which made other students laugh even before I finished my thought. They told me to sit down, and afterwards those fellow students who were always calling me a murderer attacked me. Now it was very bad; they accused me of trying to call them cats! This went on and on till the end of that semester. This developed fear in me, because not even one of our teachers encouraged me to keep on, so slowly I declined from faith.

The time came to go back home for the holidays. I knew within me that I wasn't going to return to that school, so I packed everything that belonged to me. When I returned home I learned that my uncle's wife Theresa had left and was now living in Europe, and that Uncle Baptiste was planning to

CHAPTER 6: Survivor in Exile

join her there. Then I found out that my family was alive and had survived the war in Rwanda, and that Dad had returned home to Rwanda safely and wanted me to go back.

Before I got the travel documents I went to live with Emmanuel's family in Thika, another town in Kenya. His children were my age so it was fun to be there and even stay in the neighborhood where they lived because I was able to meet other children. We had many wonderful moments to be treasured in my memory. From there I came back to live with Uncle Baptiste. Through him I learned a lot because he took me with him all times. But the time came for him to join his wife in Belgium, so at the age of thirteen I again flew with Kenya airways back home to Rwanda, my mother country, to live with my family again.

On January 24, 1997, as I arrived at Kigali international airport, I couldn't stop thinking about the misery I had been through as a refugee student and as a Rwandan in exile. But through it all, as you travel on through life, whatever be your goal, keep your eyes upon the doughnut not upon the hole! There will be a time when you can look at the past and be grateful that you made it to this day by God's grace, because you will forget your trouble and misery (Job 11:16).

CHAPTER 7
Rebellious Teenager

Chapter 7: Rebellious Teenager

In January 1997, I returned to my motherland, the country of a thousand hills. I had been a refugee in Kenya for three years. I was excited about reuniting with my family again. I knew that Mom had survived the genocide but I hadn't talked to her for a long time. My dad had returned from the Congo (ex-Zaire) forests, and my stepbrothers had arrived home from the refugee camps in Congo (ex-Zaire) three months before he did. Now almost everyone but me was back home and staying in the same house with the rest of the family members that hadn't been exiled from the country (Mom and Placide). It was only after I got home that they told me heartbreaking news about the death of my uncle Ngabonziza, my grandmother, my aunt's husband Nkusi, my friend Rosine and almost everyone in her family, and many other people whom I knew as close family relatives and friends.

This dug a hole deep in my heart, a very deep wound, a root of bitterness that grew a big stem of hatred towards God and anything related to religion. Because I knew my country was 90 percent Christian, I didn't understand *why* God would allow such a nightmare to happen. I couldn't comprehend the participation of priests, pastors, and other dominant religious figures in this massacre that left many widowed, orphaned, and homeless. This caused me to develop distrust in any professed religion, mostly Christianity. I became worry-oriented; I lost trust in people and in God.

This started out in secrets of my heart, developing later into a life bondage that could only be broken by the power of love—the only love that sets free the soul, spirit, and body. Anyway, let's just talk about the wonderful days, being back home, being back together with my mom, who had moved to stay by herself before the genocide. Truly, these were

CHAPTER 7: Rebellious Teenager

refreshing moments in our life as a family that had been previously scattered. Oh! Believe me, it was a happy reunion. I was longing to see my mother, father, and brothers. I took a flight with Kenya Airways; it seemed as though we would never get there, even though the flight was only an hour and a half.

When I arrived at Kigali International Airport, I didn't know what to expect; I had no clue who was coming to pick me up. Everything was kept a surprise. I knew I would be staying with my family, but I wasn't sure whether we still lived in the same house as before the genocide! One thing I knew for sure was that I was going to be happy again!

At the airport, my dad, my elder brother, my aunt Louise, and some other family members came to welcome me back home. I felt like a prince. As I was walking down the stairs towards the baggage claim, I could see my family from the top of the stairway; but they weren't allowed to come up where I was, and everything seemed to be taking much longer than expected. I was so anxious to hug all of them! When I had cleared everything, it was time for my long awaited hug.

As I hope you know, a hug is a great gift! It is one size that fits all, and it is easily exchanged. The first person I hugged was Dad, and then the rest. With baggage in hand we walked to the car, and I began a conversation in English with my father for the first time since childhood. Before, I couldn't even speak French, although it was a second language in our country. My aunt and elder brother knew what language we were speaking, but they couldn't speak it.

We arrived home at the house where we had lived before the genocide. It was a miracle to be home, yet the memories of why and how we left were very painful. I had had serious doubts that I would ever return again, but here I was, not only in our old neighborhood, but also with my whole family, except for those who died! The most exciting part was seeing my mother again after the long time of no hope. So many people had gathered to welcome me back to Rwanda and home. It was a big celebration; Live was back home safe and alive.

I stayed at home for a week as I waited to be admitted to a school. This brought untold disputes between Dad, who wanted me to change to the French educational system, and Mom, who argued for my continuing in English. In this case Mom won, because I was admitted to Camp Kigali Primary School, a school that had both French and English sections—but I joined the English section.

It was at this school that I met a lot of rich classmates and tried to keep up with their extravagant spending. Well, they had money and I didn't, but always I tried to show them that I had more than their parents gave them. Where did I get the money? Mom gave me transport and lunch money every day, but that is not how I used it. Instead I ate lunch at my friend Kalisa's home and I found a ride that always dropped me near our home. So, I spent the money showing off. This went on until I went to high school; then I had to go to a boarding school far from home.

In 1998, I started high school. My dad took me there; in fact, he was a graduate of the school I was going to attend. For him it was a privilege and honor to have his child study there as well. Much was expected of me since I had been accepted as one of the best students. For the first year I lived up to that expectation and finished among the best students in discipline and with high scores. Everybody liked me, but I didn't realize that I had become prideful and was declining even more from the foundations of my Christian faith to secular thinking. My

CHAPTER 7: Rebellious Teenager

concept became more and more that of an agnostic. I started protesting against God, saying that He didn't exist and that if He existed He wasn't almighty as people believed.

It didn't take much time to realize that I was mistaken. God does exist and He is almighty. As this story progresses, I will tell you how I found this treasured knowledge of God's existence and majestic splendor. He is the creator and we are the creation.

As I promoted myself and was filled with pride, I gave away to my Christian cousin Camake the Good News Bible that I'd used at school in Kenya. I began telling some of my classmates that I didn't believe in God. I explained my views by listing what I thought were hard questions about God that didn't have easy answers:

- Why didn't God stop all the killings and violence in the genocide?
- Why didn't God protect the people who were being hunted down as if they were of no value?
- Where is God when people call for His help and never get any assistance?
- Why am I still a sinner if He really can change my heart?

Along with these questions, I debated against any religion and any existence of God, drawing the conclusion that God was just an imaginary mystery and a myth. I concluded that people were supposed to live right and enjoy their lives as they wanted because life is short; we should enjoy as much as we can if we cause no harm to anyone or anything.

Since the time I started to push God away, I became a threat to myself. First, my school performance declined. I began to act inappropriately; my pretending to be rich was exposed, as I had accumulated many debts to other students. In order to pay these, I sold all my possessions, such as my mattress, shoes, and clothes, and later found myself in a deep crisis: I was left with nothing to sell! Still, I wanted to live a fancy lifestyle, so I began to steal money from my schoolmates in the dormitory. I stole the permission papers from the disciplinary office and began to sell them to students who wanted to visit their families and even those who wanted to go out to nightclubs. I became popular in the school because those that didn't have permission to go out paid me for permission slips. Some others who didn't want to go to their families would commission me to communicate with them about the problems their children were having at school. The main intention was to get them to send money to their children. Sometimes those parents gave me money to give to their children, but I would spend that money doing my own thing. Then I told the children that their parents hadn't given me anything.

Once again, consequences began to surface. The once popular schoolboy became very notorious as a common thief. I stopped going to class and simply waited for the term to be over so I could go home. I knew very well that if I ever said anything against the school I would be in trouble. So I began to plan a big lie to tell my parents to justify my failing grades and lack of discipline.

As holidays approached, I heard rumors that a meeting was to be held by teachers, as they often did at the end of the academic year, to decide on which class had done best for the year, who was the best student of the year, and who were the undisciplined that were to be sent home permanently. Without a shadow of doubt I knew I was one of the latter.

CHAPTER 7: Rebellious Teenager

On the last day as we packed to go home I didn't have much to pack, other than waiting for my transcript, which they gave me that afternoon. Sure enough, I was not allowed to come back to school. As I walked out, all I had in my mind was regret for the time I'd wasted doing things that weren't of any importance to me as a student. I reached home, but because of the attitudes I had developed I didn't want to stay there because we were poor and I couldn't eat all the wonderful food that I would buy in restaurants while at school. More than that, I wasn't free to go anywhere I wanted; my mother was very strict and wanted us to spend time reading books and doing little jobs around the house, which I didn't like. Instead I went to get a job at the cinema, where my payment was free movies and a little money.

It was at this theater that I meet a group of young boys who introduced me to drugs, such as marijuana and opium. I did not continue this new habit because I found out drugs made me do things that caused me to lose self-respect. At this point I was very afraid of living at home, because I had done much damage. I had stolen Mom's bankbooks and was withdrawing money from her account without her permission. I was using fake letters onto which I copied her signature to borrow money from family relatives and friends.

As you can tell at this point I was a rebellious teenager. I had rejected Life, and when I say Life I mean Jesus, the only one who could change my life and give me strength to overcome my sin nature and live a life that was peaceful, happy, and worry-free. I had turned my back on His love as I became more entangled in sin.

I left home to stay in different places as though I had no family. I became more and more self-centered, and all I did was focused on the present; I had no plans for future. The money I got from lies was bondage. It was spent on nightclubs, clothing, and prostitutes. Little did I know that I was heading to eternal hellfire.

One day while I was still away from home, I got the opportunity meet a football (soccer) team from Kenya who had come to Rwanda for a CECAFA tournament. They were staying in what used to be called Hotel de Diplomats, now Serena Hotel in Kigali. I was their translator and they gave me a lot of money to get them Rwandese girls, as I travelled along with them for two weeks because I could speak Swahili and English. I stayed with one Tanzanian assistant coach who always brought girls in his hotel room for sex and evening parties. This was the kind of life I adopted.

When they left I wasn't sure where to go, so I decided to go see one of my aunts in the extended family and stay for a night. I didn't know what would happen when I showed up, but that night there was a Bible study at their house and they asked me to read. The passage was First Corinthians chapter ten, and as I read, some of the verses spoke directly to me about the things that I had been doing. This got my attention, so my interest in God was restored, even though I didn't openly tell anyone. But I started feeling guilty about my wrongdoings and my rebellion towards God and my family. I made up my mind to change and decided to go back home like the prodigal son.

When I got home the next evening, Mom was already asleep, but my brothers were so excited to see me back home that they woke her up. She called to me and I went to see her in her room. (Believe me, it was quite a humbling experience!). I asked her to forgive me; she didn't say much, just prayed for me then commanded the domestic boy to cook for me. I ate and went to sleep.

CHAPTER 7: Rebellious Teenager

Dad wasn't home till late in the night. When he arrived all my brothers were watching a movie, and one of them told him that I was back home. He sent for me, but instead I got up and hid under the bed, because I thought he was going to beat me. None of them could find me, and finally my younger brother found me under bed. I begged him not to say a word but in fear of Dad he reported me. Dad pulled me out and asked me tough questions. He was very angry with me but tried to quench his anger and asked me to go into his bedroom. I didn't know why he asked me to do this; I only went in obedience, so ashamed of myself.

He came in and told me to spend the night there with him. In the middle of the night, my dad sexually molested me, which drove me some steps back in unforgiveness and resentment. I couldn't talk to anybody about this, so the next day I ran away and became a street child again for seventeen days. I went to my friends' homes for lunch and dinner, eating in a different home each time, then spent nights on the streets. Sometimes I slept on the front porches of shops with the watchmen, on pieces of empty boxes, or I would go into bars where I sat or even fell asleep in their chairs. Sometimes I would sleep in old cars parked along the sidewalk.

One night in a bar I met a drunken man who claimed to be a relative. We had never met, but he bought me a drink, french fries, and roasted beef. He was so generous even though I didn't know him. That night after everybody else left he asked the lady who served in that bar to show me the room where I could sleep. Later, that lady and that man, who owned the bar, also came into the room. Thinking I was asleep, they counted their money and stashed it in one of the jackets in the wardrobe. Early in the morning I woke up and took fifteen thousands francs, about twenty-five dollars, and went away. Nobody ever found me.

For the next three days I ate in restaurants and slept in motels. Then the money ran out! I had nowhere to go, but I found a mechanic friend who took me into his home where he lived with his Christian mom. They prayed for me and gave a room to sleep in. The next day he went to work and I went on my way, but their prayers wouldn't stop resounding in my ears. Again I decided to go home. It was late in the afternoon when I arrived at our house, and this time Mom was in her home office. She saw me coming in, and as I approached the door of my bedroom she pushed her wheelchair and came out towards the door. I couldn't look in her face. I was feeling guilty. She asked me to stop looking at the ground and look in her eyes instead.

"My son, why are you doing this to me and to yourself? Do you see how thin you are? Why won't you listen?" she begged. I couldn't speak; I just fell down on my knees and cried. She reached out with love and held my head. "I have suffered a lot for you; please stop behaving like an idiot. Accept who you are and live a humble life that we can afford; please stop ruining your life." Then she told me the story of what happened when she conceived me and how miraculous my birth was.

Honestly I couldn't stand those compassionate words. I just couldn't hold my tears back; I cried and she comforted me then asked me to take a shower because I smelled nasty. Oh! My goodness, I had never been that ugly and bad in my life. I took a shower and ate and was so happy to be home. I started to think about my life.

That evening my brothers came from school, but they were afraid of even coming near me. When my dad came home he didn't even say a word; instead he began to beat me. He asked me to lie down in the living room, and then he beat me seriously. He even gave the barbed wire stick to my brothers

CHAPTER 7: Rebellious Teenager

and commanded them to beat me at least five times each. They had to beat me with no mercy because Dad had told them that whoever showed any compassion would share my punishment. All three of them beat me very, very hard, until my mom, who was in her bedroom, called my elder brother and told him that none of them had a heart! Why would they be willing to beat their own brother? She sent word to stop Dad from punishing me further.

That night was nightmare; I couldn't sleep from the pain. My mind went through all the good times in my life with my family, recalling the beautiful memories of innocent childhood and how my rich family eventually had became poor. I thought of how I had rejected God and all the bad things I put myself through. Guilt began to come over my soul and I didn't know what to do, except to confess that I was a sinner and a rebellious teenager, whose life was a mess that only God could help and heal. I knew that I didn't love God or His salvation found in Christ Jesus, but that I needed to. This is how I came to my senses.

THROUGH IT ALL: The Choice is Rejoice

Live and Baker at Groupe Scolaire de Gahini in 1998 where I attended high school for 3 years, I was a rebellious teenager who never paid my school tuition, and it is during that time that I was molested by a fellow student older than I.

CHAPTER 8
Redeemed and Born Again

Chapter 8: Redeemed and Born Again

Since that night, I began to wonder what I had done to myself. I was once my family's favorite child, and now here I was being punished by the little ones to whom I should be giving guidance. I had been the best student, and now here I was without any intentions of going back to school. I used to be trusted by everyone, but now I wasn't even sure that I could trust myself. It was my own mistakes and the wrong choices I had made, combined with family issues and the genocide that vexed my soul. After I thought of all this, I realized my situation was hopeless and I needed an answer.

I began to think about what life would be like in the future if I didn't change! Still, I couldn't figure out what I could do to change. I knew that I needed help, but I couldn't even think of praying because I had been so disappointed by religion and those who called themselves Christians. Even though I didn't want to believe, I knew well that what William Law said was true: "He who has learned to pray has learned the greatest secret of a holy and happy life." That was exactly what I needed, so I began to attend Sunday service at a nearby Catholic church. But each time I went there I left with the same hopeless feeling and lack of prayer in my life. There was no change.

Due to my love of music, I didn't stop going to nightclubs on the weekends; I thought this was the only way to make me feel happy. It made me forget my troubles, at least for a night. One night as I sat in a nightclub, I began to think about God. A week later I was passing by a church along the roadside towards home. They were playing music, singing, and shouting. Since it was a new church and they had no building, they were meeting in a tent. There was no doors, so people could look at what was happening from outside. As I stopped to watch I felt attracted

CHAPTER 8: Redeemed and Born Again

by those young boys and girls, the wonderful songs, and the beautiful voices I heard. I decided to join the service.

My intention wasn't to become a Christian; I just wanted to listen to the choir and the music. A few minutes after I sat down, the pastor stood up to welcome the visiting preacher who had came from the UK. I had nothing else to do, so I just sat and felt the warmth of the church meeting. The visiting preacher introduced his team, one of whom was a pastor from Uganda, who was anointed and filled with the power of God. As he began to introduce himself and opened his Bible to preach, he began to say things he claimed were God speaking. As skeptical as I was, I began to question in my heart, *How can God speak through a human being?* Then he said specific things to people as he pointed out them out in the congregation. I couldn't stand to leave the church, even though that's what I wanted to do.

Then he said, "There is a young boy who has come into the service just to listen to music." Immediately I knew he was talking about me. He said, "This young man has been through a lot, and he has questions about God's existence." He went on to list the things that God was telling him about this boy—me. He described me according to the vision he was seeing, and then he said, "That boy is seated in middle section on the fourth bench."

Up to that I hadn't believed yet! I just comforted myself with thoughts that this preacher was talking about someone he knew. But when he mentioned where I was sitting and came towards me, I began to shake and feel guilty for my sins. He approached where I was seated. He said that the young boy he was talking about had even rebelled against the God who had protected him from being killed, rebelled against the God who had miraculously healed him of a terrible disease.

As this preacher said all these things, my mind relived all those events. The preacher continued to approach me, and as he got near me he said he could see who this young boy was but he wasn't going to point him out. Then he said that God had revealed all this to him to convince the young boy that it was not a fantasy, that God was giving me a second chance of life and the only requirement was that I accept his offer to be BORN AGAIN!

The preacher turned around and headed back to the pulpit. My eyes were already wet and filled with tears, because I knew that he was speaking to me. But still inside my heart I kept hearing a voice saying that I was too much of a sinner, that God couldn't forgive me. It was really a struggle! Finally I heard the preacher make a scary statement, as tears dropped down his cheeks: "Young boy, God loves you so much and will use you mightily. Come now so we can pray for you and stop the power of death that is after you. If you leave this place without being redeemed, this is your last chance. The devil has planned a fatal accident against you. You will be hit by a trailer truck."

As he finished saying those words I could not stop crying, "Forgive me, Lord Jesus!" I still don't know what happened entirely; all I know was that I was standing next to that preacher as he led me in the sinner's prayer. I became REDEEMED and BORN AGAIN. I received JESUS CHRIST as my LORD and SAVIOR. After he led me to Christ he also extended the invitation to others who were willing to surrender their lives to God, and about thirteen people responded.

Let me tell you, this has been the most powerful experience of God's presence in my life. My heart was filled with unspeakable joy. After the service people I had never met congratulated me for making an eternal choice. As I walked back home a trailer truck almost hit me because of brake

CHAPTER 8: Redeemed and Born Again

failure, but it didn't because God spared my life. Hallelujah, praise God. I went home as new creation in Christ.

Since then I started walking with the Lord Jesus. A year later I was baptized in the Holy Spirit and became more and more effective as I brought many others to Christ. I joined Bible training courses at church just to get grounded in the Word. After seven months the church prayed for us to be ministers of the Gospel of Jesus Christ, and I found that there are just two things to do with the Gospel: believe it and behave it. In the course of behaving it I went to all the people I had lied to and stolen from and asked them to forgive me. I admitted that I was a big sinner and I paid back all the money. As I did that God opened more doors for me and my life was restored, renewed, and revived.

With God, life is worth a living. I went back to school and in 2002 finished my third level of community college as third in the whole school. And God heard my prayers, because I had asked Him to take me to the best science school in our country and I got admission to join there. That's where I graduated from in 2005. At the time of my graduation, my reputation had changed; I had been nicknamed *pastor*. All this goes to show that if it can happen to me, you, too, can be redeemed and born again.

At the age 19 preaching at Pastor Justin's home fellowship in Kigali.

CHAPTER 9
Conviction or Compromise

Chapter 9: Conviction or Compromise

Being an evangelist, I have spoke in many nations, churches, Christian gatherings, and student conferences about forgiveness. I strongly believe that unity and reconciliation are a product of forgiveness. Most people think that to forgive is to never remember what happened, but that's not the way it is. Forgiving is being able to let go of the offences and hurts that people do to you and still love them as though nothing had happened. In fact, it is giving up your rights of vengeance to God. That's the power given to humans through Jesus Christ.

Well, I have learned that when you don't forgive, you lock doors on your own blessings, and that forgiving or unforgiving is a choice.

My father, after almost twenty-two years of marriage to my mom, killed her. It was daytime on September 6, 2004, around eleven a.m. On this day, one of the top-breaking news stories in my country was about my family tragedy! It was reported that a handicapped woman had been murdered by her spouse. This is as common as water is in the world, but it carries a different emotion when you know the people involved—even more so if you have a close relationship to them.

The tragedy took place at our house where we lived for ten years after the genocide that killed many members of my mom's family. My father had threatened to kill all of us, but we didn't think he was serious because most of the time he was just drunk. But no one can ever tell what is going to happen next in your life. We didn't even give it a thought, and we certainly never suspected that one day he would end up killing our handicapped mother. But it happened. The day it happened none of us children were at home because it was a Monday. My brother was at school, and I was away for three

Chapter 9: Conviction or Compromise

days in prayer. The only people at our house were Dad, Mom, and our house domestic girl.

My father sent the girl to go get our community leader, and as she arrived back faster than my dad expected, he again sent her to the offices of the sector we lived in. He knew that it would take her a long time to get there. When she left, immediately he opened the door of my mom's bedroom. She was still in the bed, and he attacked her with a hammer. As she tried to fight back he scratched her neck and hands several time before crushing her head with the hammer; then he went out and brought in two rocks. One of them was medium in size and the other one larger. Mom was struggling for her last breath when he came back into her room. She told him that she wouldn't scream for any rescue or help. He finished his murderous plan by crushing her head with those two rocks, leaving only a small part of her face. I know this because my father later confessed to me what he had done that day.

After this, he went back into the living room and sat. In the meantime, the domestic girl came back home with the leader of the community. When she told my father that the chief was there, he replied that he would meet him later and told him where to meet. Then the girl walked the chief out of our home, as the Rwandan culture is. When she returned back home, the doors to the house were all locked. She knocked but Dad didn't open. She moved around the house and went to the window of Mom's bedroom and knocked, calling my mother several times without any response. She pushed open the window and pulled the curtains aside; now she could see my mother's head bowed down. First she thought that Mom was praying, and she excused herself for disturbing her but received no response. So she took a second look to realize that there was blood all over my mother's bed. She screamed, running to the neighbors for help; when they came they couldn't get into the house, so they called the police.

The police arrived at the same time as my brothers, who had been informed about the uncertain death of our mother. My elder brother Placide was very angry and wanted to break into the house to avenge her, but the police stopped him. In the house Dad was stabbing himself with knives, so by the time the police broke into the house he was almost dead. They took both Mom's dead body and Dad, to whom they gave no chances of survival, to the hospital.

That day has remained a tragic memory. It also has become an eye opening experience that changed my whole perspective of family, friends, and even religion—since it marked the beginning of a road decorated with the flowers of hope and proof of God's ultimate protection, love, and provision. Like I wrote in the previous passages, I wasn't home at the time of the incident. The night before I had tried to go back home, but I couldn't; I had warfare inside my soul, which was trying to go home, while my spirit man told me to stay with the friends I had visited because we were praying. I didn't know why this was so! Then my struggle grew to the point at which my body began to feel weak and my backbone hurt. My friends told me to get on the bed and pass the night there. Little did I know that these pains and weakness were just a sign of something tragic: my mother's impending death!

The next morning when I woke up, I felt better but still very burdened; something was consuming my joy. I told my friends that I felt a need to go somewhere and spend a week in prayer, just to overcome the burden that I was experiencing. I took a public taxi, the common means of transportation in Rwanda, and went to the city center. From there I called Mom's cell phone; it was around 7:25 a.m. She asked me to

Chapter 9: Conviction or Compromise

come home and even told me that Dad was asking after my whereabouts. I told her that I would come after the lunch hour prayer meeting at Nkurunziza, a church in the city of Kigali. She spoke a blessing over me in our last conversation. Then she was murdered and went to the place where there are no more handicaps.

I remained in the city, waiting for the service, but because it was still early I decided to go get another cell phone SIM card to replace the one that had been stolen a couple of weeks before. It took some minutes to get a new SIM card that had my old number. It was not activated since I didn't have a cell phone. On my way back to the church, I met my friend Ghadi, who told me that he had been looking for me. He wanted to share his testimony with me about how God had miraculously opened doors for him to continue his studies in South Africa. I asked him if he was in a rush, and he said he wasn't busy at all; so I asked if he would like to join me at the church because I was going there to spend some time in prayer.

As we waited for the meeting to begin we started praying. Right in the middle of prayers I remembered that I could activate the SIM card just by placing it in a cell phone, so politely I asked Ghadi to allow me to use his. Carefully I changed the SIM cards, and as soon as I switched his phone on, it rang. It was my uncle Baptiste who live in Belgium. He asked me what had happened at home, and when I asked what he meant, in a sad voice he told me that my mother had died.

I was shocked and said that only a few hours ago I had spoken with her. He told me to go home immediately and see what was going on there, and that he would call me while I was on site.

I excused myself from the church and crossed the road to the other side to use public phone. When I called my mom's cell phone it was off; I tried Dad's, but it was the same story! Finally I called our neighbor's house; his nephew Rutahintare who lived there picked up the phone. I asked him if he knew anything about Mama Mizero (Mom's nickname). In a deeply sad tone he said they had just heard that she had died. Then he asked who I was, since I hadn't introduced myself, but as soon as I heard that Mom was dead I hung up on him. I almost lost balance, but God strengthened me. I turned around and crossed over to the other side where Ghadi was waiting. Together we went back into the church and I said to him, "Let's pray."

After we prayed I shared with him the bad news I had just received. He looked into my face as tears began to run down my cheeks, and then he prayed for God to comfort all the members of my family, knowing how difficult it was for my brother and me especially to lose such an important part of our lives—a wonderful mom, who loved, protected, and provided for us.

My own prayer was full of questions and tears. *Why? Why God? What do I do now? How are my brothers handling this? Please strengthen them, Lord, and please help me to stand strong while my heart grieves.* I remained quiet to listen and hear what God had to say, and I felt inward peace as I waited quietly for God's answer to my cry. He heard me and spoke these scriptures:

> "For my thoughts are not your thoughts, neither are your ways my ways, saith the Lord. For as the heavens are higher than the earth, so are my ways higher than your ways, and my thoughts than your thoughts."
>
> (Isaiah 55:8-9 KJV)

Chapter 9: Conviction or Compromise

> "The righteous perisheth, and no man layeth it to heart: and merciful men are taken away from the evil to come. He shall enter into peace: they shall rest in their beds, each one walking in his uprightness."
>
> (Isaiah 57:1-2 KJV)

Even though I didn't understand the meaning or see the whole picture at the time, it encouraged me because at least I knew this message was from God. It is among my principles to tackle life's problems by trusting God's promises (the Word of God), and I'm never afraid to trust unknown tomorrows to a known God.

Then I asked Ghadi to pray that I would find courage to preach and be a witness for God at my mother's funeral. As he walked me to a taxi I asked him to lend me his cell phone, which he generously agreed to. While I rode, Felicien, a family friend who lived in Italy, called me asking if what he had heard about Mom's death was true. "Was she sick? What killed her?" he asked. And he wanted to know how we were organizing for the funeral. Unfortunately I didn't have answers to any of his questions but one: yes, it was true, my mother is dead.

My home was only an hour from the city but it seemed like three. The taxi stopped at every taxi stop, letting people in and out. My heart melted within me as I asked myself question after question: what killed Mom? How is Dad feeling now? How are my brothers? Will my aunts be able to come from Europe to bury their sister? What I'm going to do? Really my heart was grieving and my mind was working overtime; my spirit man said to calm down but I couldn't. I wanted to trust God, but my heart was so grieved as I remembered all about my mother's love and care for us, all the joys and happy moments we spent with her.

By the time I got home, our house was crowded with crying women and unhappy men. All of them were in shock. They all expressed their sympathy to me as I walked in, but I didn't care. I went into the backyard, and as soon as I entered the gate I saw my mother's mattress full of blood and small pieces of her flesh mixed with smaller particle of her skull. My eyes filled with tears as I looked at the other corner and I saw my father's mattress, which also had blood spots all over it. Bed sheets were hanging on the clothesline also covered with spots of blood.

When our domestic girl saw me standing there in horror, she come towards me in tears. "Pastor," she said, calling me by my nickname, "I'm sorry about your mom."

I shook my head and asked, "Who did this? Who shot her? Where is Dad? Where are my brothers?"

"They have all gone to the hospital," she told me. "Your dad murdered your mother and he stabbed himself with six knives, so they took him to the hospital but he is almost dead."

Hearing this was like cutting my heart into two parts. I didn't know what to say or how to react. I just stood there. Finally I went back into the house and into my mother's bedroom. I saw my aunt Jacky standing there in shock, tears running down her cheeks uncontrollably. She looked at me and pointed at the wall. "Look, look what your father did!"

I looked where she was pointing and saw pieces of Mom's flesh. Then I looked down at the floor where I saw the rocks that had a mixture of small crushed pieces of bone, blood, and pieces of flesh and brain. My heart melted inside and I couldn't say a word. I began trembling so hard that I couldn't stand. Slowly I sat down on the floor, unable to comprehend that what I was seeing had been caused by my father. Honestly I

Chapter 9: Conviction or Compromise

wanted to scream, but I didn't; I wanted to cry out loud but my mouth couldn't open, so I got up walked to the room where my father slept. As I opened the door, my eyes were already wet; I was sweating and shaking. It was as if my mind couldn't process any of this.

His bed was empty; there were papers everywhere on the floor and blood spots all over the room. Seeing this, I knelt on my knees and started to pray. Yes, to pray. But why pray? Prayer opens the heart to God and is the means by which the soul, though empty, is filled with God. That's the reason I knelt to pray. I opened my soul for God to fill my life, which was so empty at that particular time because my whole world had fallen apart. I really needed God.

As I prayed God gave me a vision. In this vision I saw my mother clothed in pure white. She walked towards me and spoke to me, and she told me to forgive and love my father. She said that even though he killed her, he was still my dad and needed salvation; and as a Christian I was the one to stand and pray for God to save his soul from eternal death. Then she told me other things concerning my brother Placide before turning to walk away. I was so amazed to see her walking and not in a wheelchair. Still my heart sank as she disappeared, because I wanted to talk to her. Then I realized she was in heaven, made whole and happy. After that vision I prayed asking for the strength to forgive Dad and the courage to comfort the mourners. Now I knew where Mom was. And I knew what God meant by the scriptures He'd given me earlier.

People had been searching for me; finally one of my friends by the name of Edward called my cell number and asked me where I was. When I told him that I was at home, he said I had better come to calm Placide, my elder brother, at the hospital. Then Placide called and asked me to come to the hospital to pay my last respects to Mom before they took her into the mortuary. I didn't want to go because I knew it wouldn't help bring back Mom back, and I thought it would only cause me more sorrow. But Placide insisted, so I had to ask Allan the husband of my mom's cousin sister Monica for a ride.

When we arrived an hour later, my brother was standing together with many other people. Among them were my mom's cousin and nephews; one of them came to me and looked into my face with sympathy. I asked her where Mom was and they told me she had been already taken to the mortuary. Then I asked if she knew where Dad was.

"Yeah, I know where the murderer is," she responded. "He is being protected by the police; they couldn't allow us to avenge your mom but at least I spit on his face! Anyway, why do you care?" she asked.

I told her that I wanted to see Dad, too. She said he was in the intensive care unit. Then she said, "If they allow you to see him, just go ahead and squeeze his neck."

Placide, who was standing beside her, said, "I would have killed him if they hadn't stopped me." All this meant a lot to me; I clearly understood that they were hurt and that they really could have killed him. But things were a little bit different in my heart; I just wanted to see my dad, hold him, and pray for him; to do what my mom had told me to do in the vision. I had compassion for him, thinking that if God didn't protect him he was a candidate for eternal hellfire.

When I reached the intensive care unit I saw him lying on a sickbed covered with green bed sheets, still bleeding. He still had the spit on his face and dried blood on his neck and mouth. I reached out and held his hands, saying, "Dad, it's me, Live, your son."

Chapter 9: Conviction or Compromise

He opened his eyes and said to me that his plan hadn't succeeded. He said his plan was the only way to solve the problem. I asked him which problem, but at that point the police who were guarding him came over and asked who I was.

Dad replied that I was his son, and the police said that I wasn't allowed to be there. As they pulled me away I said out loud, "Dad, don't worry; I forgave you and I will be praying for you. Please don't try to commit suicide again. I will take good care of you."

Then the policemen drove me out and I went back to my brother and the other members of our family, who asked me if I had been able to see Dad. When they found out I had, they demanded, "Why did you let him live?" I didn't answer; instead I asked them to show me the way to the mortuary. I went with three women with whom I attended Baobab overnight prayer meetings, along with a nurse and a mortuary watchman. We opened the cold chamber where Mom was laid. When they pulled out her dead body I looked at the bandage tied all around her face, which had been seriously damaged. Honestly, this was terrifying because some of the women thought their husbands were like my father. But I still remained unshaken. As the women watched in awe, I said to them, "This is just a body; I know where the soul is, in heaven. Do you see that?" I began to quote Isaiah 55:8-9, and then I asked them to pray for Dad's soul, that he wouldn't die and that I would be able to manifest the love of God in such a time as this. We prayed and then they dropped me off at our home, where the mourners had increased in number.

The following day I visited the hospital early in the morning and went to see my father. This time I wasn't denied visitation, as he had sent for me to bring the things he needed. I visited him daily until I was able to lead him in repentance. He received Jesus Christ as Lord and Savior of his soul. This increased my joy in times of sorrow, even though my family was against me visiting him during our time of mourning for Mom.

In four days' time we buried my mother, and I got an opportunity to preach in the Catholic church where the burial service was conducted. I told everyone who attended that as Christians we are to not only forgive our enemies but also pray for them. I also shared the vision that God had given me after seeing pieces of my mom's brain on the stone Dad had used to kill her.

I forgave my father and loved him. This created a cold war between my family and me, but I think it's better to die with a conviction from God than to live with a compromise in life. So I couldn't compromise in unforgiveness. I knew what the Word of God said about forgiveness. When we forgive, our Father in heaven also forgives our sins. And we weren't told that certain sins or offences are not to be forgiven; we are asked to forgive seventy times seven. In my case this tragedy was only a chance to live the scripture. Constrained by the holy Word of God as a Christian, I forgave my father of the sexual and physical abuse as well as the fact that he had killed my beloved mother. He hadn't even apologized. I just obeyed God's Word and forgave him.

As I finish this chapter I want to ask you to do yourself a favor and forgive everybody you haven't forgiven yet. It's not hard if you allow God to deal with it.

Chapter 9: Conviction or Compromise

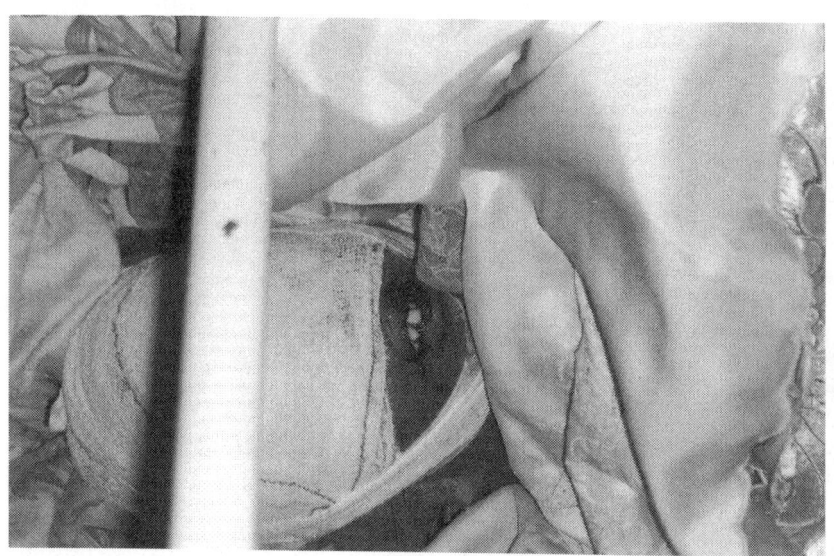

My mom's face before her burial in 2004

Live on September 6Th, 2004 the day my father murdered my mom, I took this picture after the vision I had of my mom wearing white robes, asking me to love and forgive our father for his horrible action on that day.

Chapter 9: Conviction or Compromise

From left to right Nibo Fiable, Denys Mubabo, Maxime Ngabo my cousin brother, Live Wesige and Placide Mizero on our mom's burial.

CHAPTER 10
Problems in Promises

Chapter 10: Problems in Promises

The words in the Bible are stronger than any therapy. God gives you a word that goes back into your past and heals your yesterday, secures your today, and anchors your tomorrow. The Word of God is an everlasting promise while life in the world is full of problems.

After Mom's burial, things began to change. Our dad was discharged from the hospital to an unknown place by unknown people, and nobody else cared to find where he was taken. So I began searching for him, which wasn't easy for me because it was also shameful to say that I was the son of a murderer. But there are things you can't change in life; you only need to accept the facts and keep on with what's next. Don't ever allow your parent's mistakes to overcome your personality. It is true, he was a murderer, but to he also was my father and a brother in Christ, since I had led him to the Lord.

My heart knew very well that I was at risk while searching for him. First of all, my family, especially my brothers, didn't want me to visit him. Secondly, I knew that they were spying on me because they thought I had been my father's accomplice. Thirdly, I was risking my own life because the issue of my mom's death had been made much more political; people were saying that it was a result of a genocidal mentality between Hutu and Tutsi survivors because my parents were from those two rival tribes in my country.

I searched everywhere I could possibly imagine but I couldn't trace who had taken him or where they'd put him. One day my best friend, Jean Desire, went with me to a criminal police department to inquire about Dad, and the policemen asked me what my relationship to him was. I told them he was my father, and one of them pulled out pictures of my mom lying dead on her bed, as well as the pictures of the rocks and

CHAPTER 10: Problems in Promises

the hammer Dad had used. They asked me why we didn't avenge my mom. I told them it was against the word of God. Then one of them stood up and pointed a finger at me.

"You are lucky it was your mother who died and we know how close you were to her," he said. "Otherwise you would be with your father in jail."

I asked him if he knew where my father was, and he asked, "Why do you care anyway? Your dad's flesh can't even be fed to our dogs!" Then he left. The other policeman told me to leave or I would be imprisoned.

Again I asked him to tell me where my dad was; if he did not do so, I would write to International Human Rights Watch organization and report what they were doing. Then this man pulled out a document and wrote down the number of my father's file. I was to go to the courtroom and ask for the department of high crime prisoners, who would tell me where my father was.

I was relieved to finally have this information, but my heart was also afraid. I still feared for my safety, but I went to the court. They, however, told me that Dad was at the criminal police department where I had just come from, so I knew they didn't want me to know where he was. I went back home, but I never ceased to pray and seek God for guidance.

After three weeks of this, in a vision God showed me my father's location exactly! The next day I ran into a man who knew my father; he told that he had seen him at the criminal police department and they had even talked. He told me that Dad was almost dying of hunger because he couldn't eat, and his wounds had not been healed by the time they discharged him from the hospital, I knew this was a confirmation of the vision that God had showed me. I went back home and began to pray that God would keep Dad alive and also get him out of there.

In the meantime, things in other areas of my life weren't okay. I was a high school senior preparing for finals, and I had to be at school with all these thoughts going through my head! Then when it was time to pay for school tuition, my family said they wouldn't pay for a traitor like me. So I didn't continue my studies for that year.

Things continued to worsen, until one month later someone brought a letter and gave it to my elder brother thinking that he was me. This letter was from dad, and he stated that they had transferred him to the Central Prison of Kigali. He wanted me to visit him there or else the plans we had would not be fulfilled. We really had no plans except that I had spoken with him not to commit suicide. This letter gave a bad impression and heightened everyone's suspicions that I was after something else, not just forgiving Dad. My family accused me of evil plans to eliminate them so I could be owner of all the properties. They said this because Dad had written a will the same day he killed Mom making me the head of the family instead of my elder brother.

Honestly until then I didn't know anything about this will. I explained that the only plan I had with Dad was that he shouldn't commit suicide. That night in my prayer time I heard voices at the back of our house. It sounded like three different people. I stopped praying so I could listen, and I heard them say that they wouldn't be able to destroy my family while "the praying boy" still lived! As scared as I was I began to call on the name of Jesus.

The voices left, and I went to see Placide in his room. He was asleep and I didn't want to wake him up, so I went into the living room and started to pray for protection over my family.

CHAPTER 10: Problems in Promises

As I was interceding, the light bulb in the living room burst over my head. But God protected me and not a single piece reached me. Immediately I felt an evil presence, and I began to shout and command the evil spirit to leave our house. It was spiritual warfare and I won, because the evil presence eventually left.

The next day I told my brothers what I'd heard the voices say, and on that day I went to look for prayer warriors to come and pray for our house. Returning home that day, as I approached our house I began to feel disturbed so I started to plead for the protective shield of God and Jesus' blood over me.

When I entered through the back door I saw two cats (it is commonly known in Africa that cats are used in rituals). I began to command them out of our home but instead they ran into Placide's quarters. One of them disappeared under the bed and the other one jumped out the open window. I continued to battle against it in the Spirit of prayer, and as the cat stood outside and watched me the window glass shattered and cut my finger. Then the cat ran away. I was left there praying for myself and my family.

God heard my prayers. That evening a team of prayer warriors came to pray for our house. There was a good friend Richard, a schoolmate who had been among the people that tried to preach to me before I was born again. We had maintained a strong friendship. Also, Martine, a prayer warrior and a prophet at church, came along with Tagete and Nadine, who were my Christian friends and neighbors. My brothers and I were there and we all began praying. At this moment my brothers were more fearful of demonic attacks than being angry with me.

We fought the evil spirits, commanding them out, and anointed the house and my brothers. Since then the house has been free, and my brothers were delivered from all the nightmares they were having in those days. Praise God.

Still, my brothers asked me to stop visiting my father, but I couldn't because I remembered what Mom had told me to do in the vision I had of her after her death. And Martine had given me a prophetic word of God: I should keep on visiting my dad since through doing that I would be blessed. She gave me many other prophetic words, among them that I would live in a foreign land and be used by God mightily.

But remember, where there are promises there are problems also. My problems increased one day when Placide found another letter from Dad. That was it; he squeezed my neck, choking me until I almost died. Then he asked me to choose whether I wanted to leave the house and stay away, so I could visit the murderer, or stop seeing our father and stay at home.

The sad part of this was that even my father thought I was visiting him so as to make him feel the pains of what he did, and he used very abusive word he could each time I visited. I knew he had confessed with his mouth, but it was a progressive process for him to believe with his heart, and I knew if I gave up on him he had nobody else. Although I didn't like what he said to me, I couldn't stop praying for him and even loving him. So when Placide asked me to choose, immediately I said to him that I couldn't stop what God was doing in my life. Again my brother threatened to kill me.

That night was a horrible one for me, as I thought of what was happening and how my life was falling apart. I wondered where God was in all that. I had believed Him and forgiven my dad, but it seemed since then that I was going through unexpected trials and problems—physically, emotionally, and

CHAPTER 10: Problems in Promises

even financially. I wasn't going to school and my heart was filled with grief and resentment. I began to regret my past, feel the boredom of the present, and develop a fear for the future. I knew if I didn't change something, my tomorrows would be not be fruitful.

My strength grew weak and I began to feel more and more suicidal because I couldn't see what the future held, and because I was being persecuted on both sides. I lost hope, and belief only seemed like a fantasy. The next morning I made up my mind to commit suicide. I thought it would put an end to my problems, since the only person who cared—my mother—had already died. I couldn't think of anything good that had ever happened to me; the devil had convinced me that I was a nobody in the world and that nothing good would ever happen in my life; he also convinced me that if I died nobody who hated me would trouble me anymore.

Around noon I got an electric extension cord and plugged it in in my room; then I bought mineral water in a bottle, which I planned pour into the electric plug in and then tie myself with the extension cord to be killed by the electric shock. Everything was in order.

As I prepared to kill myself, I became very thirsty and began to drink the water in the bottle. Then I remembered it wasn't for that purpose that I had bought it. I stopped drinking and began to say my goodbyes to God. A telephone call interrupted me; I had forgotten to switch off my cell phone. It was a lady I had prayed for who had been barren for nine years at the time I met her in one of the prayer meetings where I had preached. The power of God was present in that meeting, and I gave her a prophetic word that she would give birth to a baby boy. Well, this was the call a year later, right on the day I was going to put an end to a life I hadn't even created.

She had called to say she was coming home from the hospital with the baby boy I'd prophesied about, and that they wanted me to come to their house on the weekend to dedicate the baby.

Well, God does offend the mind to reveal the heart. I had witnessed the power of God, and I knew He would deliver me if I trusted Him. But here I was on the edge of committing suicide. After she hung up I began to ask myself who would lose if I died, only to find that it would be me. So I made up my mind not to commit suicide but to trust God to help me *through it all.*

I surrendered to God. I repented of having such evil thoughts and decided to pray and seek God in my problems, because I knew there were many promises for me. I went to a family that owned a mountain house. I had known this family before my parents died; they were Christians and I frequently visited them and attended prayer meetings in their house every Friday. The wife of this family, Monica, was one of the three women who had gone with me to the mortuary to see my mother's corpse, so it was amazing how God put us in contact way before they realized that I was one of the two orphans they were told to adopt in the prophecy.

They were a rich family who owned a hotel called Baobab, and they also had a house in the mountains. I asked them to permit me to stay in their mountain house for some days because I wanted to fast and pray in repentance. I went there and began my prayers. I neither ate nor drank, and on the fourth day God spoke to me: I heard the voice of God to my heart. It told me to stop worrying and to trust Him, and He would restore my life. He would give me another family, He would give me a sister to replace the one who had died in the

CHAPTER 10: Problems in Promises

genocide, He would take me to America and use my life to touch many people.

That same day in the evening, the family that owned that place came to spend some time in prayer with me. At the end of the day I went back with them to their home. I didn't feel much like a visitor there because I had been attending overnight prayer meetings in their house previously. I stayed for two days as I waited to regain strength after the four days without food. Then I told them that I would go back to pray on the mountain.

This time they told me that as they were planning on visiting their children in the U.S., I could stay at their house and pray as much as I wanted. They even told their son to give me transport money anytime I wanted to visit my family. Little did I know that this was going to be the family that God had said He would give me! They went to America for a month, leaving their sons, the hotel staff, and me in charge of the hotel business.

God tremendously blessed us in that month. And there was a revival going on, as workers gathered four days a week to pray along with the sons, myself, and Jacky the domestic girl. I visited Dad anytime I wanted and took him food from the hotel. I thanked God for His love and divine way of provision for me.

A month later the family returned and I began wondering where I would go now. But God had something else planned; Stanislas the father and owner of the hotel came to me in the morning and asked me what we had done while there were gone. I didn't know why he was asking me the question, so I began to guess; my reasoning was that someone had stolen his money and now I was going to be questioned for that. But before I even said a word he told me that it was a miracle; that he had owned that hotel since its first day in business but they had never made such profit as we had in a month. *Hallelujah! Hallelujah!* My heart shouted within me, because now I understood it wasn't anything bad. Then this man said to me that I was like Joseph because the Bible states he was rejected by his brothers just as I was. He smiled at me and said, "I want you to stay here with us."

"Glory to God," I said began to weep—not because he had asked me to be his son but because this was a confirmation that God had heard my prayers on the mountain. This man, whom I soon began to call Papa, told me how in 2002 God had sent a prophet into their home to tell them they would adopt a young boy whom God was using, and it so happened that while they were in America God told them that I was that young boy!

Stanislas also told me to go home and get all my things and then to come live there with his family. Then he asked me if I would like to go back to school. I said yes and he gave me all the money I needed to get back into community college. Hallelujah, praise God.

I will share more about my new family, and about God's hand of provision through it all, but let me end this chapter by telling you that little trials without God will break you, while even big trials with God will make you great. It is through trials that we learn to seek and depend on God, hence the growth of faith in Him. Remember, what is impossible with men is possible with God. And in the world there are problems but in the Word (the Bible) there are promises. If you are in happy moments praise God; in difficult ones seek God; and in painful moments trust God because His promises are like the stars—the darker the night, the brighter they shine.

CHAPTER 11: Minor Details of Life

This picture was taken at the prayer mountain of Rebero after Friday prayer meeting. It is here I went to pray for four days fasting and God told that He would bring me in USA, the people in the back ground attended prayers there every Friday, with Stanislas Sibomana, Aline Umugwaneza, Monica Sibomana and Live Wesige

This picture was taken on my dad's funeral In Muhura at my Grandmom's house where we buried him in 2005. From left to right Placide, Live Wesige, Denys Mubabo and Fiable Nibo

CHAPTER 11
Minor Details of Life

Chapter 11: Minor Details of Life

When God becomes your focus of living, He will make you living evidence of his faithfulness; and if you worship Him, tomorrow's situation will be a new adventure. Then when God touches you, those who used to ask "who are you" will change to "how are you?" Just hold on to God and never let go of all the wonderful promises from the Bible of God for your life.

I had been living with my new family for a few months when they adopted yet another orphan, Aline. She became the sister I had lost. My family had rejected me, but it was all right because now God had given me a new family that took care of me in everything that I ever needed. I was going to school, and they paid for my transportation and school tuition, doing everything possible to help me in my daily struggles. I visited my father as much as I wanted to, and they provided for everything that he needed. I never forget that before my father died, Papa (Stanislas) and I went to visit him at the hospital.

Once, a close family relative told my younger brothers that I was a nobody and worthless, and that it would be pointless to invest a dime in my education. He counseled them not to follow my example. But when good things began to happen, he heard what God was doing in my life; he changed his tune and helped spread rumors that I had become rich and left home to stay with the rich! He said I didn't love my siblings and even that I was living with a widow. Whenever I visited my brothers, they tried to get me back home, but my new family, knowing what could happen, counseled me not to. Moreover, it was too late; God had already promised me that I would live in Papa's family till I came to the U.S.

Things were a lot better for me in my new family. But my dad's health declined because they discharged him from the hospital before he was well. He was having difficulty breathing

CHAPTER 11: Minor Details of Life

because of lung problems, and his living conditions were not conducive to good health so he became weaker and weaker. When my friend Jean Desire visited him in prison, they spent a considerable time talking about God's love. Dad taught Jean Desire a gospel hymn.

Since Dad's new occupation in prison was praying, worshiping, and praising God day and night, whenever I visited him we would talk more about God's love. When my dad was ill, the prison put him in the Central Hospital of Kigali. One Wednesday afternoon on the way to visit him I met Hakizimana, the co-coordinator of Victory Fellowship of Rwanda, a Christian group that I belonged to. Hakizimana accompanied me to Ignas's restaurant. Ignas's family were good friends with my new family; they were devoted Christians, too. While my dad was ill they always gave him free meals, since the hospital was near their restaurant. Aimee Hakizimana also bought soft drinks, sugar, and powdered milk for my dad to use while at the hospital.

Then we visited Dad at the prisoner's block; the guards were nice to us and let us in. My dad was glad to see my Christian brother with me, and he began to testify how my loving and forgiving him stopped him from committing suicide even after his first attempt; and that God used Christian love to give him a hope for his life. He told us that he was very sure of eternal life because he'd taken this second chance as an opportunity to cleanse himself of all evil and sins. He'd asked God to completely wash him in the blood of Jesus.

Just a week before my dad died in October 2005, I visited him at the hospital because he was very ill. When I saw him he was seated in a wheelchair, and tears flooded my eyes because I saw an image of my mother in him. Then I remembered what the scriptures say: we reap what we sow.

When we sin we can repent, but there will always be a time to face the consequences of our sins. In my father's case he was to sit in a wheelchair just like Mom and wait to be helped by someone else.

My father looked in my eyes and said, "Come, and I will teach you a lesson of life. We entered the prisoner's block, where he took me to greet a woman who was once a state minister in my country and our neighbor before the genocide. She was lying on her bed and she no longer had any honor; her body and face were in a poor physical shape and she wore prisoner's uniform. But she was excited when we greeted her and prayed for her.

Afterwards, Dad asked me if I had learned any lesson. When I asked what he meant, he said to look at him. Tears began to run down his cheeks and he said to me, "Son, that woman was once a famous person. She had everything it took to be called rich and prosperous, just like myself. I have visited many countries in Europe, I lived a life of plenty and owned worldly things, but that's not what life is all about. I despised poor people but I became poor myself, and now I understand that anything can happen and that whatever goes around comes around; what you sow is what you shall reap. The Bible is true when it says that a man's life consists not of the things he possesses. If people were humble enough to acknowledge that God is the Master, the one and only Creator of the universe, then they would find fulfillment.

"Son, the lesson I want you to learn is that the world has nothing to offer. But if I died today I would be content and glad because I have found the real meaning of life. It is to give my soul over to God for His salvation."

Then he told me that he regretted what he did—not only killing my mother but also how he'd wasted time and all the

CHAPTER 11: Minor Details of Life

riches God had blessed him with. Then, looking at me he said, "Son, keep God in the center of your life and let Him be Master over everything that you will do. Then you will be successful. And please try to get your brothers and everyone you come in contact with to live Godly lives."

As tears filled my eyes, my father told me that he had read through the whole Bible and was confident he would not go to hell, neither would his spirit burn in the lake of fire. He had accepted Jesus as Savior and Lord over his life. He held my hands and we prayed before I left; a week later he went to be with the Lord.

On the day he died, I was with Papa (Stanislas) and his youngest son Arthemon. I had asked Papa for a ride to the place where I was going to preach. On the way I received phone call from my uncle Dieudonne telling me about my father's sudden death. I couldn't cancel the meeting, so I went ahead and preached, sharing my dad's testimony. It touched people, and many received Jesus as their Lord and Savior. At the end after I prayed for them, I mentioned that on my way I had received a call informing me his death. So I asked the congregation to pray for my family and me. From there I went home.

My uncle had brought Dad's body into our house. Nobody was at home when I got there, and I stayed there for almost two hours before anybody came just because their hearts were still angry with him. Later some of my classmates and Christian friends came, people who were bold enough to help arrange the funeral disregarding what my father had done a year ago.

Dad had asked to be buried at his mother's house, and with true friends I drove miles away from our house to his home in the village. It was raining so heavily and the ground was so muddy that I thought nobody would come! But when we finally got there I was surprised to see numerous people from his village, people he had helped there. I got the opportunity to share Dad's testimony and preached a little, then led people in prayer. On his burial day people got saved and received the Lord Jesus as their personal Savior. Hallelujah to God!

After the funeral was over, my brothers were crying, guilty of not having reconciled with him before he died. This became another open door for me to minister to them about forgiveness and the love of God. Although I become victorious, still my dad died at a bad time for Placide and me. We were only few weeks away from doing final national exams, completing high school, which is equivalent to community college in the U.S.

We came back into the city that very night. I slept at home, and that day my brothers apologized to me. I told them that I had already forgiven them. The next day I went back to my new family for some time before going to stay at school to prepare for the exam. Although I didn't succeed, my heart was comforted by the encouraging words of Stanislas and Monica, who didn't give up on me even after I failed. Instead they kept on trusting and loving me.

For the second time, they went to visit their children in the U.S. and left me in charge of the hotel and home. This time even my adopted sister Aline, the other orphan, was gone to school in South Africa; so I stayed home alone for two months. I was in touch with my new family through e-mails and phone calls. They even sent a friend to represent them at my party to celebrate my salvation birthday. I celebrated seven years of being thankful to God for the marvelous things He had done in my life.

That day over two hundred people came and helped me to celebrate, and five got saved and received Jesus as their Lord and Savior. Among them was Placide, my elder brother. I want to quote his words on my salvation birthday: "I never thought

CHAPTER 11: Minor Details of Life

my brother would be somebody whom people would even consider a friend, or that they would come to join him as he celebrated the victory of the cross over sin in his life. After all, here I am to witness that God has really turned my brother's life. At first we all thought he was faking, but he kept on getting deeper into the things of God. Later, when our mom died, we thought he was crazy, for he easily forgave Dad, who had killed her. But today I realized he has found the secret of better living, and I want to be born again."

Hallelujah, I was so excited to hear these words coming out of his mouth. Oh! It was so wonderful; the presence of God was all over that celebration, and we laid hands on him and prayed for him together with those others who been born again. Later all the people prayed for me and we gave God the glory by singing and dancing before Him until midnight.

Time passed and my new parents returned, along with Aline who finished her studies in South Africa. At this time God told me through prophecy that my time in Rwanda had come to an end. I was to prepare to go to America for further studies. Even though I knew it was His will, it was hard for me to see a possible way for this to happen because of everything I needed in such a short time. But in life we need ignorance and confidence; then success is sure. So I ignored the fact that I'd failed the national exam and had no certificate of completion of high school. Still, I gained confidence in God and I trusted that He would make a way for me. Anyone can count the seeds in an apple but only God can count the apples in a seed. I trusted God, for He alone knows what's next in my life.

Through it all I learned that no one could ever discourage me. In my new family we had missionary visitors who came and went. Sometime we organized seminars and conferences for church leaders, and invited missionaries from the U.S. and other nations to come and train those church leaders and even evangelize in their churches. Because I translated for them, I traveled often with them as they preached all over Rwanda and its neighboring countries. I enjoyed it because I knew I was waiting for God's timing for me to move to the next level in my life.

It was during one missionary conference in October of 2006 that my brother came to see me at the hotel where I was working as a translator. Placide told me that he had come because he was concerned for my future. He asked why I hadn't gone back to school to repeat so I could sit for the exam and at least have a certificate, instead of staying there doing nothing but always running behind white people and translating for them when none of them cared about my future. He told me that I must go back to live with them at home.

I sat there looking at him; then I said, "Stop worrying." I reminded him that I wasn't living with Papa because he had chased me out of the house and even threatened to kill me, but because God had a plan and a purpose for my future. Then I said to him, "Look, God told me not to go back in school here in Rwanda. He will take me to study in America."

Placide stood and said, "You have put your future in danger. You were once a brilliant boy but you will live to regret this choice."

I immediately realized he had backslid, because he pulled out his cigarettes and began to smoke as he went out. I went back to the conference and translated as if nothing was wrong, but my heart was desperate. I was interceding that God would prove my brother's words wrong.

I shared this with Aline and we began to seek God, praying for doors to be opened for us to get scholarships in the U.S. We even asked our other siblings by adoption to help us. But regardless of

CHAPTER 11: Minor Details of Life

how much we tried, it was all in vain. We applied to study at Christ for the Nations in Texas, but their reply was a big NO.

The missionary team from Australia which I had been translating for was getting ready to leave, but before they left God spoke to Pastor Malcolm Taylor, who was the team leader, and told him to pray for Aline and myself with the domestics at Papa's house. As he prayed he began to prophesy to Aline and me to get ready because God's time was at hand for us to come into the U.S. It was a confirmation that God had heard our prayers and answered them.

Staying in one of the rooms there was an elderly lady, Susan, who had come from the southern province to receive Jesus. She was 104 years old! That evening, since I wasn't busy, I decided to go talk with her. As we were exchanging a wonderful conversation she told me that God was speaking to her, and she asked me to remain silent! After a few minutes she opened her eyes and said to me that she saw a team of eight people, most of them white American, coming to this house—with my blessing! I thought this might be the answer to my prayer.

Just two days later, we were surprised by a call from Uganda. It was Pastor Emilio, who was getting ready to cross the border coming to Rwanda, and he was with a team of missionaries from the U.S.! Everybody is always welcome at Papa's big house. The team arrived—exactly eight in number, and all except one were American. The team members asked my sister Aline about her testimony, and Connie, the wife of Pastor Claude Tyler, was very touched. They promised her a scholarship to their Bible college, leaving her in Rwanda to await their invitation to the U.S.

This was so amazing because prophets had been prophesying to her to get ready to come. In March of 2007 she got her visa and traveled to the U.S. together with Monica

(Mama). But I was left behind, and my best friend Jean Desire had gone to South Africa to study, so I began to seek God, asking what was wrong with me that kept me from receiving my promise. God said that nothing was wrong but that I had to wait for His timing. I began to confess the Word, which says to call those things that are not as though they were—regardless of many the challenges, because I didn't have any contacts in the U.S., I didn't know who would pay for my plane ticket, and I even didn't know whether I would be given the visa.

After two months the same family of Pastor Claude and Connie Tyler invited me also. They paid for my tuition to come in their Bible college, where I would attend the ISOM (International School of Ministry) program for two years. God provided the visa, air ticket, and pocket money. And on May 28, Placide escorted me to the airport and told me, "Your God is mighty. He can do miracles for those who believe and patiently wait upon Him." I told him that he needed to repent and believe in God for everything.

Coming to the USA was a prophecy fulfilled, and it taught me that *nobody* could became *somebody*. As you are just one chapter a way from the end of this book, I want you to know that if you have been told you are nothing, just ignore that and tell yourself that God can get something out of nothing. A nobody might also be somebody in the future. So be nice to people on your way up because you will meet them on your way down. Now God has used me to help my family in Rwanda, and all those who mocked me during my time of waiting are now ashamed of the bad things they said against me. Because where others see a shepherd boy, God sees a king.

CHAPTER 11: Minor Details of Life

Front low Aline Umugwaneza and Terry Tracy at the back low from left to right David and Donna Matejcek, Pastor Claude and Connie Tyler, Maureen, Monica , Pastor Rally, Stanislas, John Hakizimana. This is the missionary team that Susan told me about.

Left to right Pastor Claude and Connie Tyler, Aline Umugwaneza, Miss Scarlett, Live Wesige, Papa Stanislas, Dr Berin Gilfillan on my graduation from International School of Ministry in 2007.

CHAPTER 12
The Choice Is Rejoice

Chapter 12: The Choice Is Rejoice

Life is a challenge: meet it.

Life is a gift: accept it.

Life is an adventure: dare it.

Life is a sorrow: overcome it.

Life is a tragedy: face it.

Life is a duty: perform it.

Life is a game: play it.

Life is a mystery: unfold it.

Life is a song: sing it.

Life is an opportunity: take it.

Life is a journey: complete it.

Life is a promise: fulfill it.

Life is a love: enjoy it.

Life is a beauty: praise it.

Life is a spirit: realize it.

Life is a struggle: fight it.

Life is a puzzle: solve it.

Life is a goal: achieve it.

Much is said about life, but less is said to define what life really is. As a young man I know less about life, but as a Christian I found out more and I can easily define life just like

CHAPTER 12: The Choice Is Rejoice

Dag. H. described it as follows: "Philosophy theorizes about life. Psychology analyses life. History records life. Sociology classifies life. All men desire life. If life is a comedy to he who thinks, and a tragedy to he who feels, it is victory to he who believes in Jesus Christ." But Jesus said, "I am the life."

There were so many times that proved the fact that my life was in the hands of God. Tell me who else could have stopped those lions from eating my mother and elder brother. Tell me who could have stopped the plan to abort me—if not God!

God has the utmost authority in life. He knows every minor detail of our lives. Let me share with you some of the things that amaze me. If you had seen my father, you would easily recognize that I'm his son. One day during the genocide after we had been scattered, I hid with my younger brother in a home near the roadblock where many people passed going in the city. My dad passed by and didn't know where we were, but the soldier there had seen me, because he had almost killed me the day before. When he saw my dad he knew he was my father just by looking his face, and brought him where we were hiding. That was how we met up with our dad, just because my face resembled his, especially the ears! Ha! You see, that's what I mean; God knows even the minor details of our lives.

Here's another example. Back in my country I used to get up early around three o'clock and go through the streets preaching the Gospel of Jesus Christ. Many people heard my voice as I walked through their neighborhoods. One day I needed sixty thousand francs (one hundred dollars) for my father's blanket, mattress, bed sheets, and other necessities in prison. I tried everything I could to sell my cell phone to get the money, but I couldn't find a buyer. Then Olivier, an ex-classmate told me that his mother Josephine wanted to meet me because they had heard me preaching. So I went with him to meet his mother, who told me that God had laid it on her heart to give me some money. She gave me an envelope with the exact amount that I needed.

In 2003 I was on an airplane traveling elsewhere for further studies. But when I reached Kenya they stopped me just because the Rwandan passports had been changed. They urged me to go back to Rwanda and get a new passport. As upset as I was, I stayed in Kenya, thinking that our embassy would help me; but they told me that they only helped those who had residency in Kenya. So I had to go back in Kigali. It was so humiliating and embarrassing to go back into the country after all the goodbyes and the farewell party. However, I remembered my friend Samuel had told me that even though I was going, there was still a lot to be done at home; he told me that God had sent him to give me that message. Guess what? When I returned to change my passport it took three weeks to get a new one, and when they gave a new passport somehow they kept my old one that had my visa in it. When I asked for it they told me that it was burnt by mistake within other old passports they had burned. So I had to start the whole process of applying for a visa over again!

All this was very upsetting because they acted very slowly that I began to worry and blame God for the disappointment. People began to say that I'd lied, that I didn't have the visa and there was no journey. But God knew what was ahead, because in the course of waiting for my new visa my dad killed my mother and also tried to suicide himself. If I had gone it would have been difficult for me to understand such a tragedy. Nor would it have been easy for me to get the airfare to fly back for Mom's funeral and burial. It also wouldn't have been possible

CHAPTER 12: The Choice Is Rejoice

to lead my father into repentance and becoming born again. Hallelujah to God, who always knows every minor detail of life.

After I was rejected by own family I thought isolation and suicide would be an answer to my problems. But that would have caused me to eternally perish. When I trusted God with my future, He gave back everything the devil had stolen from me. God knows even the number of hairs on your head. He knows when you comb how many falls, and He cares for you (Matthew 10:30). It is your responsibility to trust Him with the unknown future and quit worrying. When your attitude is right, there is no barrier too high, no valley too deep, no dream too extreme, and no challenge too great for you.

As I write this book I live with David and Donna Matejcek, whom God has used to care for and host me not only in their house in Michigan but also in their hearts and family. They have encouraged me to write this book and even made DVDs of my testimony. They have prayed with me throughout, because it wasn't easy to relive the past as I wrote this book. But if it weren't for God who knows and cares for minor details of life, there would have been no chance that I would have ever met this wonderful couple.

The first time I saw them was back in 2006 when they came to Rwanda for missions. They were among the eight missionaries who came to Rwanda—remember the words of Susan, the old lady in the previous chapter? Although they stayed with the family that had adopted me, we didn't get a chance to talk because I was busy translating for the whole team and they were also busy all day, going to churches to minister. Little did we know that one day I would be living at their house with them. Oh! They have accepted me as family, and I have beautiful memories of them. But was it our plan? No! It was God's.

THROUGH IT ALL: The Choice is Rejoice

Donna and David Matejcek, Aline Umugwaneza and Me at home in Michigan.

CHAPTER 12: The Choice Is Rejoice

I remember that four days after I landed in the U.S., Pastor Claude and Connie Tyler, the hosting family living in North Carolina, were taking a trip to Michigan, so we went with them and all stayed at the Matejcek home. That was how I met them again. I remember that David, Claude, and myself went up north to visit and help Pastor Claude's sister Ruth, and there I got an opportunity to really talk with David.

Ruth had to attend a Wednesday service at a little church in Grayling, Michigan, called Burning Bush Tabernacle. The senior pastor was Patricia Petrie. We went with her that evening, and that was the first church that I ministered to in the U.S. When I got up to share my testimony, the glory of God filled the place. I ended up praying for the people and they blessed me. One lady told me that I should write a book, and then a man said I could even make a Christian movie based on my testimony. Wow! This was just a short conversation, but what an eye opener! I will never forget another lady who said to me that she had just been revealed something about my name! She said, "Your name is Live—live in victory every day—and that's the message God has for you." So I'm trying my best to live in the victory of the cross in my life.

The next day we drove back to Flint to David's house where Pastor Claude held a prayer meeting in the basement. He asked Aline and myself to speak, and few days later we went back to North Carolina, little knowing that we would be back to live with the Matejceks. But at this point God was putting together minor details towards our reunion, which happened few months later.

While in North Carolina God told me to accelerate my ISOM studies and complete them, which I did; in fact I graduated a year and a half before the estimated time, so I began to ask God, "What next?" I left North Carolina to visit a branch of our church in Africa, and there God guided us to come to Michigan. While we were still wondering *where* in Michigan, Donna and David Matejcek called and invited us to come over and live with them as we searched for scholarships to further our education. That is how we ended up living with them, and how I ended up writing this book because I had so much time.

Now I can write and speak English. Again, it is because God knows every minor detail of life. In 1994, when I became a refugee in former Zaire (present D.R.C) with my father and young brothers, I got terribly ill; but when I got well my father for fear I would die sent me to live with Uncle Baptiste who lived in Bukavu. We all left Zaire and later went to Kenya. All this was bad in some ways, but God has His way in every detail of life, according to Isaiah 46:10. No one ever thought that I would need English in my life, since my country's second language was French, but God took me to Kenya where they spoke English and Swahili. Learning English there enabled me to translate for many missionaries who came to Rwanda after the genocide, and now I use English in everyday life.

Life is composed of many minor details that work together to make what we see with our eyes. The inner workings of the human body are living proof that we don't see outwardly how we might hear, see, smell, touch, and taste. Whatever else may be said of man, this one thing is clear; he is not what he is capable of being if he trusts his mind only, which he hasn't seen, yet fails to trust God, who has created his mind. That's the reason why we fail to solve the puzzle of life.

Though it all I have learned that the reputation of a thousand years may be determined by the conduct of one hour, so we should never lean on our own understanding. Instead we should surrender our being to the Giver and

CHAPTER 12: The Choice Is Rejoice

Author of life because He knows every minor detail, whether past, present, or future.

So, to conclude, I want to advise you to never say never to God. He has good plans for your life. I shared much about my story, but again in this chapter I intend to share with you three important things to avoid. I have discovered that many mistakes I made were as a result of these three things; also I have seen many fall in the same trap. No matter what age you are, it will affect you if you fall into the lifestyle of:

- The regrets of the past.

- The unfruitfulness of the present.

- The fear of the future.

Before I share with you how I learned about these three things, I will say that every person has a past, a present, and a future. We all begin our past in the same way, as a little seed inside a mother's womb (Job 10:11). Then we live in seconds, minutes, hours, weeks, months, and years as part of our present. Finally, our future is again the same, as it is held in the hands of death—physically and live for ever spiritually (Psalm 90:10).

The Regrets of the Past

What is in the past cannot be changed. The past is here today and gone tomorrow; it never comes back. And that is the way it is in this life. We were created in a way that we live on one side of the road of life, each moment walking through experiences that come together at the end of life to form our reputation. Each moment you breathe, whether in a second, minute, or hour that makes up time, it is impossible not to be affected positively or negatively either by people or circumstances—even your own decisions. That's what makes memories.

As I'm growing, I realize most mistakes that I made were because of this terrible error that only human beings commit: forgetting that there is a Creator who brought the universe into existence (Psalm 146:5-6) and that one day either in this life or the life after each will give an account of our actions here on earth.

We all have the same beginning, birth, and it is at this point that we realize that life has an Author (Psalm 139:13-14). If we were wise enough to stop and wonder at the creation of a baby inside a mother's womb, we would learn the lesson of trusting God with our life and its unknown future. The fact is, however, that many of us don't marvel at this great miracle, which the rich and the poor, the educated and the uneducated alike share (Proverbs 22:2). We put ourselves in positions of regretting what happened to us in the past, blaming others for what they did or didn't do and condemning ourselves for the things we did or didn't do. Instead, we should be thankful that God helped us through the challenges and around the obstacles.

We have to triumph over our past tragedies. Maybe you were born into problems and grew up in the absence of one or both of your parents; maybe you have lost everything valuable you had; maybe you have been married many times without any success; may be you have been unfairly charged and are now serving punishment for a wrong you didn't commit; or maybe you did wrong and now are suffering the consequences justly. Maybe you have never been loved and cared for by anybody; maybe you have an incurable sickness; maybe you have became widower, widow, or orphaned; maybe you have nobody to trust; maybe you have dealt treacherously all your

CHAPTER 12: The Choice Is Rejoice

life and now are no longer trusted; maybe you got yourself into addictions of some kind and it's hard for you to break free; maybe for different reasons your education has been put on hold, etc.

In all this, people, circumstances, or even our own choices can be the factors leading to such outcomes, but there is no sense in regretting what you can't change. If you can only manage to conquer your thought process and surrender all to God, who created you and deserves your worship, then through it all He can make a way of escape for you (1 Corinthians 10:13).

Had I leaned on my past there would have been no way to become a better me. Happy as I am today, I have lived in situations that could have caused me to build prison walls of self-pity. Instead I have found a way of escape, avoiding the regret of a past I can't change. Please use your time well, as it's the only asset you have; and remember that today well lived will be happy memories tomorrow. Forgive others for the things they did or didn't do, and forgive yourself. No matter your past, don't regret it but learn from it; otherwise it will give birth to an unfruitful present.

The Unfruitfulness of the Present

The flowers of tomorrow are in the seeds of today. This means that whatever you need to see changed or done tomorrow, now is the best time to prepare for it.

My mom once told us (my brothers and myself) as we were gathered around her in her bedroom that she suffered regrets of the past till early 1990. My dad had remarried her younger sister, and she thought that she was left on earth for nothing but suffering and to be called useless. But when she began to

THROUGH IT ALL: The Choice is Rejoice

seek God and put her hope in Him, quietly waiting upon the salvation of the Lord, her life began to dramatically change.

First a friend gave her a book to read in her loneliness. As she read she became inspired by the story of how the author, a handicapped woman, had overcame struggles and became successful. My mom made a decision that she wasn't going to allow the past to interfere in her present life. She didn't want to spend the rest of her life unfruitful, even though many were the challenges she would face. She could no longer walk, her beloved husband had turned away from her, and she had lost her job and was doing nothing other than sitting at home and complaining about everything that wasn't happening in her favor.

But she never gave up. Instead she took on a project and asked my dad to invest some money. He refused to support her business plan, but she didn't lose hope; instead she borrowed from the bank and built a small workshop at the fence of our house compound. Later she bought sewing and knitting machines to equip the workshop, which was how she began a tailoring and knitting business. God blessed her with skilled workers and she got many customers; then my father's wealth began to decline while hers increased. In fact, after the genocide Mom's business was able not only to provide for our home needs but also paid for our schooling.

I don't think she would have made a difference by sitting around and complaining. But most people who are not even handicapped allow themselves to spend the rest of their lives doing nothing but complaining. This will not change anything; get up and began to look for what you can do! Never say never, as long as you live.

CHAPTER 12: The Choice Is Rejoice

The past almost ruined my life by adding many unfruitful habits to my future. During my teen years, especially my second year as a senior in high school, I thought it was the time to be free and do as I please. I stayed on campus away from home. I joined a group of alcoholics who also were chain smokers. We were never involved in any profitable school assignments; most of the time we stayed in dormitories talking about girls, food, outfits, and new songs, as well as playing cards and learning different dance styles. We were busy all the time doing nothing fruitful while others were in class, doing their homework, or studying.

The time came for me to go home, and we had to take report forms to our parents. I was so ashamed of my class performance and didn't want my parents to see my report form. So when I arrived home, I did all my best to avoid any conversation relating to school. I begin to wake up early morning and go to play basketball or soccer so that Mom wouldn't see and ask me for the report. Every time I came back home I told a lie.

Little did I know that she already knew about my report form because my brother had accidentally found it and showed it to her. From that time I lost her confidence in me. See, not only did I lose credibility but my reputation at school was affected; at the end of that academic year I was demoted instead of being promoted. And I didn't like that, so I dropped out of school. Then, if you remember, my life became a mess.

You can always pick up the pieces and move on; you are not so heavy that God cannot lift you up. All you need is to let go and let God. If you bring Him into your life He will restore and renew your strength and help you through your present so that you don't continue being unfruitful. Don't allow a day to pass by; use every second being productive for God and your life. Don't do things you might regret after a time, and stop pushing things that you should be doing today to a future day you really don't have.

The Fear of the Future

Mostly the fear of the future is a product of the unfruitful present. See, most people live in fear of what is going to happen—not because they have reason to be so afraid but because they know and live their past in the present.

It is the same reason that leads to many other horrible mistakes; abortion in some cases is a product of fear of the future. Sometimes, when people fail to find a solution to upcoming problems they have, fear of the future drives them to drink, drugs, prostitution, theft, all kinds of killings, and many other forms of bitterness.

Even the devil himself is afraid of his future; that is the reason he is always trying to deceive as many people as he can, so they can share his eternal judgment of living eternally in hellfire. See what fear of the future can do?

Here is how you can avoid the regrets of the past, the unfruitfulness of the present, and the fear of the future. You should *look backwards with gratitude, upwards with confidence, and forward with hope* (read Lamentations 3:21-25).

I don't know what you have been through or what you are going through. But these things are true about life: no matter where you are in the world, no matter your gender, religion, education level, how famous or notorious you are, how careful or careless you have been—if you lack the understanding of this reality then you will never choose to rejoice. Please take these three things into your soul, spirit, and body:

CHAPTER 12: The Choice Is Rejoice

1. It is common.
2. God is faithful.
3. There is a way out.

1. It is common.

Know that what you go through is common unto men and that you are not all alone. Someone else somewhere is going or has gone through the same things you are. This should be in your mind before you begin to pity yourself.

Don't hang yourself because you lost your job, house, parent, or sibling; or because your partner has left you. Don't hate yourself because you never had parents or siblings, never went to school or graduated, never gave birth, never got a good marriage—there are so many other causes of this deception: wars, hurricanes, floods, earthquakes, fires, famine, and tragedies in which human life and property are lost. Maybe one of these greatly affected your life. The truth of the matter is that it is very hard for you to bear the pain of losing such valuable things and people. Yet still it is common. How you react to what happens is what makes the difference.

Don't try to find happiness and fulfillment in things that can endanger your life, such as prostitution, drugs, smoking or drinking, and premeditated murder. None of these will solve a single problem regarding what you are going through. You just need to tell your mind that it's okay to go through it and that it's common.

Let me list two things that are common: birth and death.

Birth is not your choice; you don't choose what family, country, or continent you are born into. Birth is a living proof of life after death. It would be hard to explain to a baby inside the womb that there is life after birth, even though we all know there is. Likewise it is hard to explain to us that there is life after death. But believers know beyond a shadow of doubt that life continues after death.

Birth is common, God's miracle that we all can be witnesses to.

Now for death. It is very hard to find a topic that people all over the earth agree to without complications, but death is one hundred percent sure. But we should also remember there two kinds of deaths: physical and spiritual. Both are eternal.

No matter who you are, you have a debt to pay to death. Sooner or later you will die. I hate the idea, but it is a reality. Do you wonder why physical death exists? It is because the wages of sin is death. And we all have sinned. Physical death is inevitable, but spiritual death is a result of your choices here on earth. Your very life is like a seed in your hands. You are responsible to plant it in the ground of God's Word and let it die to self so that you may live eternally with God, bearing more life. Spiritual death is avoidable if you surrender to God.

2. God is faithful.

If you were once a child and now you have grown, there is no need to explain to you that God does exist. Your very life is a living testimony proof of God's existence. Look at it this way. You can trust your ideas, which you have never seen or touched, because you are able to touch the products of your ideas. So why is it so hard to believe in God, whom you will meet at the end of this life? You cannot see or touch Him, but you can see and touch what He has created, including the air you breathe.

CHAPTER 12: The Choice Is Rejoice

If you have read my testimony in this book then you can really say God is faithful. He can guide us and show us His goodness. He has showed me his faithfulness since my birth. During the genocide, His mercies made ways for me while I was a refugee, and He has shown me His kindness even when I thought my life was over.

You will never be happy in this life until you have learned to put your dreams second to God's purpose for you. Are your tomorrows in the hands of God? Who owns your future? Surely all of us have questions and anxieties about our future. But God holds the future in His hands. He will not let you down. He is a friend that sticks closer than a brother.

3. <u>There is a way out.</u>

The darker the night gets, the sooner the morning comes. Some people have been in situations too terrible to imagine, just like myself; I didn't know if I would ever be happy again! But God does have ways of escape for everything we go through. My birth story is a testimony of His way of escape when the doctor failed to come to the hospital. If you have read what I went through in the genocide, sure enough you know the several ways of escape that only God could make for my life.

I don't doubt that you have life experience of a similar kind. I hope you can testify that in your life God has often made a way of escape to get you out of a mess that you sometimes created yourself.

It has been wonderful to walk with you through the journey of my life. Now I hope you will join me as I spread the message behind this whole book to everyone on the face of the earth, and tell them that THROUGH IT ALL, THE CHOICE IS REJOICE.

Remember life will bring pain all by it's self but your responsibility is to create joy, as you choose to rejoice, the bible says and I quote "Rejoice in the Lord always; and I say, Rejoice. Let your moderation be known unto all men. The Lord is at hand. Be careful for nothing; but in every thing by prayer and supplication with thanksgiving let your request be made known unto God" –Philipian4:4-6.

Made in the USA
Charleston, SC
09 April 2012